1st Edition

Monkey See, Monkey Don't

See Why 88% of Real Estate Agents Fail.
Don't Be One of Them.

Alysse Musgrave

HelpUBuyAmerica.com/Dallas, Houston, Austi

Monkey See, Monkey Don't. See Why 88% of Real Estate Agents Fail. Don't Be One of Them. 1st Edition.

ASIN: B00BF69Z0O ISBN-10: 1522748784 ISB-13: 978-1522748786

To caffeine and sugar, my faithful companions.

"You can't look at the competition and say you're going to do it better. You have to look at the competition and say you're going to do it differently."

—STEVE JOBS

TABLE OF CONTENTS

Preface

The streets are littered with the bodies of Realtor®s who came and failed before you. Why, why, why is the failure rate so staggeringly high? There are *dozens* of books that try to teach you how to succeed in the wonderful world of real estate. There are *thousands* of websites referencing the subject. Brokers offer new agents incredible opportunities for training. Still, more than 88% of new agents are out of business within two years. Why? The number "1.7 million" has a lot to do with it. I'll explain this later. But why in the world do so many of us jump into the business when the odds of success are stacked so greatly against us?

In a word, freedom. Freedom to set our own schedules. Freedom to raise our own kids and keep them out of daycare. Freedom to be responsible for our own destiny, and freedom from the oppressive, stifling, mind-numbingly boring world of corporate America.

I'm a 2nd generation Realtor. My Mom wore the mustard yellow Century 21 blazer for many years before she switched to commercial real estate. Although I worked several summers in her real estate office, I had absolutely no desire to become a real estate agent. None! It was Texas A&M for me, not the Houston Community College School of Real Estate. HCC doesn't have a football team, after all.

So how did I get here? I blame my daughter, Lia, and Diane Keaton. Lia is to blame simply because she was born; she was (and still is) the cutest, sweetest thing I had ever seen. I couldn't tear myself away from her. Diane Keaton gets the blame because she made a movie called Baby Boom, which is about the struggles women face when they have to choose between having a career and being a Mom. That movie made me think more about entrepreneurship. I had already been investing in real estate for a few years when I learned of a new form of representation called "Exclusive Buyer Agency." I'm a terrible salesperson, but I'm a great caretaker; I was a natural fit for this type of business.

For 20 years, I have been protecting the rights of homebuyers. It's been intrinsically and financially rewarding, but I have not been without my critics. The attack on my business model and me started almost immediately after I put the EBA sign in my yard. My slogan, "Don't Let Them Make a Monkey Out of You!" offended some people. And, as you can imagine, I didn't make a lot of Realtor friends when I started using a monkey on my business cards in lieu of an actual photo of myself. I guess I brought that hate on myself.

The hate, and even threats (yes, threats!), continued when I spoke out against predatory lending practices very publicly in the late 1990s. In 2012, I tweaked my service offerings and my already successful business exploded. As a consequence, the hate now comes from my own people. According to one Exclusive Buyer's Agent, there are "special places in hell" for people like me who offer programs that deviate from the norm. That's a bit harsh, don't you think? Are we such a tightly knit, communistic members-only club that there is no room for alternative business models? Apparently, we are.

I love real estate, particularly the math and the negotiations, but I don't really like calling myself a real estate agent. In fact, I find most commission-based industries to be distasteful. My personality is not a natural fit for the aggressive world of sales. I would never approach someone in a restaurant and hand him or her a business card, or go door knocking to market myself. I'll help you buy a house, and I'll do a great job, but you're going to have to come to me. But it frustrates me that the world of real estate and its players are not open to bold new ideas. Just try and promote a new concept in this business! Traditionalists, young and old, will come at you with a vengeance. It's like throwing raw meat in the middle of a pack of starving dogs! *Toe the line. Don't be different. Starve like the rest of us.*

No thanks. Toeing the line is not what I do.

It is my hope in writing this book that other agents will embrace my business model and that they will work with me to offer truly unique services to homebuyers across the state of Texas and across the country. That's my goal. I know I'll never convince all of you that my way is better, but I'll convince some of you. That is good enough for me.

A word to the agents who will send me hate mail after reading this book: Don't. It's time to embrace change. The world of real estate is not immune from change brought on by advancements in technology. You might hate change. You might be afraid of change. But you still have to live with change. Along with the change comes opportunity. Think outside the box and don't be afraid to ruffle some feathers. Who cares if the Realtor down the street doesn't like you! You can't sell them anything anyway.

Read with an open mind. And even if you decide this business model isn't for you, I guarantee you'll learn a few new things that you can use to foster the growth of your existing business.

About This Book

It's been said that a good nonfiction book conveys to the reader only the necessary information – and not one word more. That doesn't happen here. Still, the focus of this book is fairly narrow.

The first section is a lighthearted look at the public's perception of Realtors. I warn you, it's not pretty. We'll look at the convoluted way that the real estate industry is structured and the effect this structure has on both consumers and agents.

Next we'll learn why so many agents fail in this business. We'll walk in the shoes of a brand new Realtor and watch her try to navigate all the organizational and financial traps that have been set for her. Then, we get to the meat of the book. I'll present what I believe is the easiest, sanest, most respectable path to success with your real estate license. Your income will be stable. You'll feel good about your job and maintain control of your life. It's all the things you love about real estate and none of the aggravation.

What follows is the training guide that I give to my own agents. It's a step-by-step guide that will teach you the proper way to represent homebuyers. Exciting? Not really. It can be technical and boring. But, in theory, you can read this book and launch your career as an Exclusive Buyer Agent. *In theory*. The responsible thing to do after absorbing the information in this book is to spend some time with a home inspector, a loan officer, an appraiser, and a title company. There is only so much you can learn from a book. On your own and by yourself, go look at about 20 houses. Pretend you have a buyer, and follow the steps outlined in this book. At the same time, work on your marketing plan and your branding. By the time you are comfortable with construction, pricing, the software, etc., you'll be ready to hit the ground running. Should you decide my way isn't the right way for you, there's still plenty of useful information here that you can use to enhance the quality of service you already offer to your clients.

This book follows the procedures that we use in Texas. Each state has their own laws and policies, and it would be impossible and irresponsible for me to address them all here. These differences, however, don't detract from the message and value of the information contained in the chapters ahead. You will easily be able to adapt this information to comply with the laws of your state.

To thank you for buying this book, I welcome you to contact me at Alysse@HelpUBuyAmerica.com with any questions or comments you have about the material presented here. I'm always happy to help. Enjoy!

{ 1 }

Greedy, Immoral, Scum-Sucking Pigs

According to Reader's Digest, real estate agents are number five in their list of most distrusted professionals. In case you're curious, number one was a psychic and number six was a lawyer. Ouch. LoveMoney.com also has real estate agents at number five; car salesmen are number four on their list. Generally speaking, the world views real estate agents as greedy, immoral, scum-sucking pigs.

I went online to try and understand why people feel this way, but what I read did little to either clarify the issue or ease my pain. In fact, the level of animosity made me consider nursing school. Nurses, by the way, are the most loved and trusted professionals.

I found this rant on IsItNormal.com. The anonymous author has some pretty strong feelings about Realtors! The grammatical errors aren't mine.

"I hate Realtors.

Realtors are the most self-serving dishonest useless 'profession' I've ever encountered.

Before the internet people needed Realtors. Otherwise you were stuck with classified newspaper ads and yard signs. Back then they served some kind of purpose. Today they've been reduced to nothing but a list (MLS).

Now let me tell you how I really feel about Realtors. Realtors are near obsolete lying worthless useless self-rationalizing crooks! Not to mention the profession is a dime a dozen. ANYONE can get a Real Estate license.

REALTORS ARE CHEERLEADERS. You don't need a Realtor to buy or sell a house. Realtors were the retail pushers of the housing bubble and foreclosure crises, which has taken the United States to the brink of bankruptcy. Realtors produce nothing. In GENERAL Realtors are extremely arrogant. Realtors constantly pretend that you need them. Their smug arrogance says, "You need me. I don't need you. I have the keys to your house". I hate this profession with a passion! Let me tell all the Realtors reading this page something:

1) Your NOT Doctors

2) Your NOT Lawyers

3) Your NOT Financiers

4) Your NOT High Powered Investors.

YOUR JUST ANOTHER GODDAMN REALTOR!

When someone tells me they are a 'Realtor' I instantly lose respect for them.

REALTORS ARE SCUM. Why did the average person depend and trust in these so called 'professionals' to provide them transparent, unbiased and correct information in all aspects of the housing process? How can Realtors look at themselves in the mirror knowing they are nothing more than professional liars and cheerleaders who facilitated this foreclosure mess and debt crises our country now faces? How can someone have a CONSCIENCE knowing they intentionally pushed a grossly overpriced houses on family's knowing full well they could not afford the payments in 10 months and would be kicked out? Not everyone was a speculator or betting the market would go up. Most people just wanted a home for their families! How can you live with yourself knowing what you did? You lied and self rationalized to GET YOUR 6% COMMISSION.

The NAR has even tried to push censoring county property websites and Zillow to gain selective discloser advantage. Real Estate has got to be the only business I know where the buyer can SEE the entire sales history of the property/house at the county records website and Zillow.

As I said the only card Realtors have left to play is the Multiple Listing Service (MLS). When that is eroded away by discount brokers and integrated FSBO websites, Realtors will surely go the way of the travel agent. Buyers and sellers worried about paperwork can take confidence in the fact these procedures can be completed yourself at a fraction of the cost by a Real Estate Attorney. A Real Estate Attorney is more knowledgeable and will do a better job than a Realtor at a FRACTION OF THE COST. And unlike a Realtor, the attorney truly does work in your best interest."

Here's what someone commented to this poster's rant:

"Realtors are nothing but needless and unnecessary parasites that get far too much for doing close to nothing. They mislead people trying to create the impression that they are determinant and necessary in the path towards home ownership and lock them into

stupid contracts and terms that basically limit their choices and options."

Brutal! Surely, I thought, the posters mentioned above were extreme in their thinking. I decided to put my theory to the test. I went online and posted the question, "Why do people hate Realtors?" Here are the answers I received. Again, the grammatical errors are not mine.

- *"We all hate people who steal, cheat or otherwise are ethically or morally challenged."*

- *"6% for doing very little other than listing a property.. is one big reason.."*

- *"Because they do hardly anything for the crazy amount of money they get. As housing prices goes up so does their fees, and they're not doing anything more. Sellers like myself resent it. There should be cap."*

- *"They keep trying to pawn off bad homes on buyers that they want to get rid of."*

- *"It's the fact that this business makes many agents sneaky and greedy. Some of my former and current friends have become sneaky when they started that job... really strange..."*

- *"Because they know them."*

More pain. Maybe, I thought, I asked the wrong question. I tried again and asked, "What do you think about real estate agents?" Here are some of the responses:

- *"Please, I'm eating."*

- *"Because they show me $400,000 houses when I can only afford a $300,000."*

- *"They are sales people posing as "agents".*

- *"Hate them because they can't be trusted."*

Hmm. I began to wonder if real estate agents around the world were hated as much as American agents. Consumers around the world were asked, "When I say the word real estate agent to you, what word comes to mind?" Here's how they answered in Melbourne:

- *Crook*

- *Dodgy*

- *Swarmy*

- *Be careful*

- *Pushy*

- *Scumbag*

- *Don't trust them*

- *Charming. They know how to work the system.*

- *Sly and sneaky*

- *Shady*

- *Wicked vulture*

In England, real estate agents are "snake oil parasites that would stab their nans for a fiver." And "Estate agents aren't short of a trick or two. In fact, they have an entire treasure chest full of them, which is often encrusted with Krusty the Clown's mug shot."

So, the worldwide consensus seems to be that real estate agents are worthless parasites, unworthy of love, friends, health, or happiness. Nice.

There is Scientific Evidence That We Are Scum!

Chapter two of the book Freakonomics, by Steven D. Levitt and Stephen J. Dubner, is entitled "How Is the Ku Klux Klan Like a Group of Real Estate Agents?" Their claim is this:

> "A phrase like "well maintained," for instance, is as full of meaning to an agent as the code phrase "Mr. Ayak" was to a member of the Ku Klux Klan; it means that a house is old but not quite falling down. A savvy buyer will know this (or find out for himself once he sees the house), but to the sixty five year old retiree who is selling his house, "well maintained" might sound like a compliment, which is just what the agent intends. "

According to the authors, the real estate agent writes deceptive ads and then just waits for the right buyer (read: sucker) to come along to purchase the property. Clearly, these authors have no idea how the real estate system works in this country, and I'm not even sure what point they are trying to make. I do know that I don't like my occupation being used in the same sentence as the KKK!

The Butt of the Jokes

Then there are the real estate jokes. Here are a few good ones:

Q: What's the difference between a real estate agent and an accountant?
A: The accountant knows he is boring.

Q: Do you know how to save a drowning real estate agent?

A: Take your foot off his head.

Q: What is the definition of a good real estate agent?
A: Someone who has a mortgage loophole named after him.

Q: Why was the real estate agent so excited that he completed a jig-saw puzzle in only 9 weeks?
A: Because on the box it said 8-12 years.

And these are my all time favorites:

First Agent: Did you pass your ethics exam?
Second Agent: Yes, I did! Of course, I cheated.

How do real estate agents traditionally greet each other?
"Hi! Nice to meet you. I'm better than you."

Even Jimmy Fallon makes Realtor jokes. In his "thank you notes" seg-ment, he says, "Thank you, real estate brokers, for earning thousands of dollars for saying 'How about that one?'"

I don't mind being the butt of the joke, as long as the jokes are funny.

Why All the Hate?

The bottom line is that real estate agents have failed to prove their value to the consumer. But let's look a little closer at some of the reasons cited for all the hate.

"It's the fact that this business makes many agents sneaky and greedy."

This statement isn't even an implication. It's "the fact," they say, that seemingly nice, normal law-abiding citizens become real estate agents and suddenly become so motivated by greed that they abandon their moral code at the expense of the consumer. It's "the fact!"

Um, hardly. I've been a Realtor for more than 20 years. In this time, I have encountered lazy agents. I have encountered untrained agents, and I have encountered burnt out and even incompetent agents. But I have never encountered an agent who was a thief or a liar. A puffer? Yes. An aggressive sales person? Sure. But a liar and a thief? Nope. I do believe that there are real estate agents out there who are unscrupulous, and I know a whole bunch of agents who are annoying. In fact, some people consider my monkeys annoying. But the vast, vast majority of real estate agents are not thieves. That's a fact.

> *"Before the internet, people needed Realtors. Otherwise, you were stuck with classified newspaper ads and yard signs. Back then, they served some kind of purpose. Today, they've been reduced to nothing but a list (MLS)."*

Here's a partial list of what a listing agent does for their client:

- Properly price the home
- Stage the home for sale
- Review title information
- Measure the property
- Confirm the lot size
- Take photos and videos (or pays someone to do so)
- Put a sign in the yard and a lockbox on the door
- Coordinate showings
- Create marketing brochures
- Perform open houses
- List the home on the MLS

- Deliver feedback to the clients
- Evaluate all offers
- Produce net sheets for the sellers
- Counsel seller on the offers
- Confirm the buyer's qualifications
- Ensure the earnest money contracts are fair to their seller
- Coordinate inspections and repairs
- Deliver the survey and HOA information
- Schedule the appraisal
- Etc., etc., etc.

The Orlando Area Association of Realtors compiled a list of 184 activities that a listing agent performs!

Here's a list of what consumers think a listing agent does:

- Put the home on the MLS
- Spend their commission check on fancy cars & vacations

Clearly, consumers don't understand what we do nor do they value our services. As an industry, we spend too much time promoting our accomplishments and not enough time promoting our services.

"They keep trying to pawn off bad homes on buyers that they want to get rid of."

Not exactly. Sellers hire real estate agents to help them sell their property, and some of those homes are dogs. A lot of them are dogs, actually. But listing agents are being paid thousands of dollars to present "bad" houses in the most positive light possible. That's how you sell homes.

Here's an ad we would write if we were telling the truth about some of the houses on the market today:

"This place is a dump. It smells like feet, and it looks like frat boys lived here for 30 years. I hope someone buys it before the air conditioning and appliances die. Hopefully we won't have a storm that destroys what's left of the roof and fence. 24-hour notice required to hide the dirty dishes and clean the cat box. Call (555) 123-1234."

This ad would generate nothing but lowball offers from investors, and most sellers have no interest in selling their home for 50 cents on the dollar.

Should an agent turn down listings that aren't in pristine condition? Of course not. Their job is to get creative, generate interest, and ultimately procure a sale. Some would call this creativity "puffing." I prefer the expression "putting lipstick on a pig." Doing the job that we are being paid to do is not fraud.

"As housing prices goes up, so does their fees, and they're not doing anything more. Sellers like myself resent it. There should be cap."

Like it or not, there is some truth to this. Yes, as the size of the home increases, so do some other expenses. The cost to photograph a 9,000 square foot house, for example, is much higher than the cost to photograph a 2,000 square foot house. The same is true for inspections, staging, and sometimes appraisals. But the amount of work the Realtor must do to sell a $500,000 house and a $200,000 house is the same. In fact, if we were to be paid based on effort, our commission would be higher when we sold a less expensive home. First-time homebuyers are a lot more work than more sophisticated buyers who have experience buying and selling homes and who have worked their way up to a luxury price range. Advertising expenses don't vary based on the price of the home. A two-inch ad costs the same regardless. And it's no longer necessary to place ads in upscale publications to attract high-end buyers; the Internet is the great equalizer. More than 85% of homebuyers begin their search online, not in the newspaper or other magazines you might find at the car wash. A homebuyer isn't going to walk into Re/Max and ask to see their menu of homes for sale. Marketing a home today means putting the listing on the MLS; the MLS feeds into Realtor.com, Zillow, Trulia, and other sites.

Consumers resent agents who don't at least acknowledge the fact that they don't have to do a whole lot more than list their home on the MLS in order to generate interest in their property and ultimately a sale.

A listing agent's value is not in their ability to list their client's home on the MLS. Any monkey can do that.

Their value is in pricing it properly, selecting the buyer that is truly ready, willing, and able to purchase a home, writing a contract that protects the seller's interest, etc. Realtors need to do a better job spreading this important message.

"How can Realtors look at themselves in the mirror knowing they are nothing more than professional liars and cheerleaders who facilitated this foreclosure mess and debt crises our country now faces?"

This is a really big accusation and, unfortunately, a lot of consumers believe this to be true. Are Realtors really responsible for the foreclosure crisis? It's more accurate to say that we all share some responsibility – Realtors, loan officers, appraisers, and homebuyers. The path to homeownership does allow opportunities for fraud. But where does the responsibility of the Realtor begin and end?

As Realtors, we can tell a buyer that he or she might be fine with a $200,000 house, yet they fall in love with the $300,000 house. Are we responsible when they default on their loan? No. But we do have a duty – as professionals and as moral human beings – to warn them against being house poor.

Are Realtors responsible for the activities of the subprime lenders? If a B or C paper buyer comes to me pre-qualified to purchase a $200,000 home, am I to turn them away so that they work with my competitor down the street? No. But it is my responsibility to make sure that they understand the terms of their loan.

If a listing agent lists a property for $350,000, but I determine the value to be $300,000, am I at fault when my buyer's appraiser okays the sales price at $350,000? Nope. But it is my responsibility to tell my buyer they are over-paying for the house.

A system of checks and balances does exist in the real estate world. A proper appraisal protects both the buyer and the lender from an artificially high sales price. Properly trained Realtors can protect homebuyers from the practices of predatory lenders. The great housing crisis of 2007 to 2011 is complicated and beyond the scope of this book. But for Realtors to be named the villains is absurd.

Perception is Reality

When a buyer or seller reviews their closing statement, all they see is the $8,000 commission their agent is being paid. What they don't see is the 35% broker fee that comes off the top ($2,800), the 32% you send to Uncle Sam ($1,664), and the other expenses you incurred like gas, the coffee or lunch you bought them, or the money you spent on software, lockboxes, marketing, etc. (assume $500). Now, your $8,000 commission is $3,036. A trip to Bermuda? Sure, if you don't have to pay your mortgage or buy groceries. That's your reality. Their perception is you just put $8,000 in your pocket and that you probably have two or three other suckers closing this month too. You're rich!

The bottom line is that a large number of people perceive Realtors to be greedy, lazy, and immoral. Try as you might, you'll never change their minds, and it's a waste of time to try. Their perception is our unfortunate reality, and it's really our own fault. Competition is fierce in this business, and in an effort to differentiate ourselves from the agent in the next cubicle, we use phrases like "Millions Sold" or "Chairmen's Club" or "Platinum Club" or "Top Producer." In Dallas, you can buy an ad in D Magazine and claim to be the "Best Realtor" in your area, and you can bestow this honor upon yourself for the low, low price of $3,000. You can also be in the "Who's Who in American Real Estate." Our credentials are meaningless to the consumer, particularly the buyer who doesn't want to be "sold" anything. But in a desperate attempt to differentiate ourselves from other agents in our area, we spend money we don't have to earn our GRI, CRS, ABR, e PRO, AHLS, and EIEIO.

Here's the big problem: There are very few ways for a Realtor to stand out in this industry. So, traditional agents spend more and talk louder than the next guy in the hopes of getting noticed. Real estate is a 'fake it till you make it' business. And the more money you have to fake it, the faster you'll make it. No money? You can still make it, but it's going to be a lot harder and take a lot longer, and it may never happen. Doesn't sound appealing to you? Keep reading. There's a much better way.

Why Would Anyone Want to Be a Realtor?

Here are the answers I received when I asked, "Why did you become a Realtor."

- "I love people and making them happy."
- "I like educating the clients & seeing their faces at closing."
- "I love being able to help people and enjoy a lifetime of friendships with all of the people that I have helped find their homes."
- "I was ripped off by a Realtor once and I wanted to make sure this never happened to anyone else."

Not true. Here are the real reasons people go into real estate:

- You don't have to go to a 9-to-5 job and spend hours in traffic.
- You want to raise your own kids.
- There is the potential to earn a lot of money.
- You don't know what else to do and your neighbor, the Realtor evangelist, recruited you into his company.
- You put your career aside to raise your kids and your skills are no longer marketable.

Yes, it can be rewarding to see a young married couple close on their first home. You hand them the keys, and the handsome groom carries his lovely young bride over the threshold. But if you've ever helped someone buy a home, you know it doesn't work this way.

In the real world, the buyers are dazed and confused because they don't really understand the process and they aren't 100% sure they can trust you. Sellers are overwhelmed with vacating their old home and moving into their new one. It's been said that the top three most stressful life experiences are death, divorce, and moving. Sounds about right, but I would add handing your teenager the car keys to the list.

If you want to have a successful career in real estate, start by being honest with yourself and others. You got into real estate for the lifestyle and the cash. There is nothing wrong with that! It's the American dream, and it is highly, highly achievable – if you do it right.

{ 2 }

Mass Confusion

How did we get to be one of the least-respected and most-hated professions in the world? It doesn't matter. I'm not a big believer in looking back in
order to look forward. I don't want to write about the history of real estate
any more than you want to read it. We are where we are, and it is what it is. If
you want to earn a living in real estate, you have to find a way to work within
the confines of a system that doesn't always function in ways that benefit
either the consumers or the agents. But let's take a look at some of the things
that don't make sense to anyone but us.

Dual Agency

Dual agency is the concept of serving two masters by representing the
buyer and the seller in the same transaction. The broker collects a double

commission, calling into question the integrity of the entire transaction. A dual agent cannot get the highest price for the seller and the lowest price for the buyer at the same time. It is simply impossible.

Dual agency is illegal for all other professions and is considered fraud in every other industry. But real estate brokers are exempt from liability for this fraud, and the consumer's risk on one of the largest transaction of their lives remains ridiculously and unnecessarily high.

The large brokers rely on double-dipping to stay in business, and states have adopted various schemes to disguise this fraud. The terms "intermediaries" and "designated agents" are just other names for dual agents. The public is overwhelmed and confused by all of this, and the concept of dual agency is one reason that consumers think Realtors are crooks.

Commission Based on the Sales Price

There is nothing inherently wrong with commission-based occupations. These jobs exist in every corner of the economy, from real estate agents and stockbrokers to car salesmen and contractors. When a company wants to push their sales team to work hard, they pay through commission. It's a classic, proven strategy, and it works.

From a seller's perspective, however, it's no more work for a Realtor to sell a home that costs $300,000 than it is to sell one for $330,000, yet it costs the Seller an extra $900 in real estate commissions. Fair? Not really.

How about buyers? Is it more work to help a buyer purchase a $500,000 house than it is to help them buy a $200,000 house? Nope. And how can you trust a Realtor to negotiate the lowest price on your behalf when they are being paid based on the sales price of the home? It's a leap of faith. Buyers will always be at least a little suspicious of your motives, and rightfully so. Therapists have no incentive to make their patients well. Lawyers have no incentive to settle the case. Car salesmen will sell you a lemon to earn a commission. And Realtors will always "….stab their nan's for a fiver."

We're Too Expensive

It typically costs a homeowner $18,000 to sell a $300,000 home. That's a lot of money! From a Realtors perspective, it's all about risk/reward. The higher the risk, the higher the potential reward, and Realtors assume a LOT of risk. Seller's agents have to pay to photograph, videotape, and promote a client's home for months, sometimes, to sell the house. If the Seller changes their mind, the Realtor doesn't recoup those expenses. Buyer's agents typically show dozens of homes to a buyer before they make a decision. We use our gas and risk our own personal safety by putting strangers in our car and taking them to empty houses. In the end, we're not guaranteed a paycheck. Our reward is a lifestyle that is in our control and a nice paycheck if we're successful. Sometimes we work for dirt, and sometimes we work for diamonds. But in the consumer's mind, we're always overpaid.

Business Arrangements with Vendors

Each party to a real estate transaction is supposed to be unbiased and independent in their work. Appraisers are to verify the value of the property, inspectors are to find defects and verify its condition, and the title company is to verify the chain of title and underwrite a title policy. The system of checks and balances is disrupted when the real estate broker has a business relationship with the title or mortgage company, for example, or if the home warranty company is paying the Realtor a fee to send them business. These behaviors are technically legal with proper disclosure to the parties involved, but are still "icky," and it puts our integrity into question in the eyes of the consumer.

Realtor Bonuses

"Secret" bonuses are commonly offered to selling agents who bring the buyer to a particular house or builder. Accepting a bonus calls into question the credibility of the persons involved in the transaction, and is yet another reason why people don't trust Realtors. How would you feel if the person you trusted to help you make one of the most expensive purchases of your life were to be given a kickback? You wouldn't like it. In my mind, there is no justification for this behavior. You simply can't act as a fiduciary for your client and later take a bonus, especially when the buyer only learns about it at the closing table.

We're A Work in Progress

The real estate industry has definitely evolved. Not long ago, Realtors were not even required to disclose to the public whom they represented. Can you imagine having a conversation with a lawyer, only to find out later that he or she represented the person who was suing you? Sellers did not have to disclose to the buyer anything about the condition of the property. Lenders could get away with increasing their prices by thousands of dollars the day before closing, after it was too late for the buyer to back out of the deal. None of these things are now true. The real estate industry is a work in progress, but we've come a long, long way. It's a much safer world in which to buy or sell a home than in days past. There is still a ton of room for improvement, but I believe we'll get there.

{ 3 }

We're So Annoying!

Like it or not, we contribute to our bad reputation. Don't believe me? Visit Trulia or Zillow and read the responses Realtors are posting in the "advice" pages. As an industry, we do obnoxious things to try to gain a competitive edge over the agent in the next office. I cringe with embarrassment when I see some of the following in action.

Shameful Marketing

Although it feels like there's a Starbucks on every corner, there are actually only 13,000 locations in the United States. By contrast, there are roughly 1.7 million active Realtors chasing the same buyers and sellers. That's stiff competition! And in an effort to stand out and get noticed, we do some crazy and often humorous things! I've seen ads with Realtors posing with their pets, in witch costumes, a team dressed as characters from the Wizard of Oz, and even Realtors under water holding up sold signs. Hilarious. We do what's necessary to earn a living, I guess. But we sacrifice our dignity along the way. I include myself in this statement.

Constant Bickering

I hate when I visit real estate sites and find Realtors bickering with other Realtors. The name calling, bullying, and one-upmanship are an inexcusable embarrassment.

Recently, a buyer posted a question on Trulia. They had been working with their Realtor to buy a house for the past four months, and their lease was set to expire in about seven weeks. Their agent's son was graduating from college, and the agent made plans to attend the ceremony. Mrs. Buyer was very upset that their agent was 'abandoning' them when they needed him the most, and she wanted to know how to get out of her buyer's representation agreement with him. Unbelievable. The responses to this buyer's question were unbelievable as well. Although the other Realtors should have come to the defense of this agent, they tried to steal the business instead. Wow! Should the agent skip his son's college graduation to spend the weekend being at the beck and call of these miserable buyers? No, of course not. There is nothing wrong with being a Realtor and having a life. But for 20 agents to respond with ways for this buyer to fire their agent is pretty disgusting in my mind. We're being paid like doctors and lawyers, but behaving like thugs. It's a disgrace.

Too Much Ignorance!

Continuing education classes exist for a reason. Laws change. Procedures change. As real estate professionals, it is vitally important to learn and understand changes that may affect our clients. I find that agents from the big brokerages do a good job of staying on top of changes in the industry, but independents have a tendency to let things go. Not only do you put your clients at risk when you aren't aware of legal updates, you put yourself at risk for lawsuits. Take your continuing education classes seriously and pay attention!

PIDOOMA

In an effort to appear more knowledgeable and experienced than they really are, some agents engage in a practice I call "PIDOOMA," or "Pulled It Directly Out Of My A#*." Stop it! There are at least a dozen people involved in any given transaction; it's not your job to know how to underwrite a loan or produce a closing statement. Become an expert in your chosen specialty, and then surround yourself with others who are experts in their own field. Don't try to be a master of all trades. You'll make a fool of yourself.

Now Is a Great Time To Buy!

It's not always a great time to buy! It's *usually* a good time to buy, but not *always*. And some people should *never* do anything but rent. Making these blanket statements to try to encourage buyers to jump into the market hurts your credibility and reduces you to cheap salesman status. When you take on the role as advisor and consultant, the buyer has more faith and trust in you. Isn't that what you want? Adopt a "do the right thing" attitude and buyers will be lining up to work with you.

Cold Calling/Door Knocking

I know that large brokerages strongly encourage their agents to make cold calls and knock on doors, and I've read that door knocking is effective. From a work ethic standpoint, I can admire someone who has the nerve and drive to go knocking on doors. But in my mind, it's desperate. It tells me that this agent has nothing better to do than go out there and beg for business. Aside from the image it projects, it's just annoying when someone calls or knocks on my door to try to sell me something! A working, busy agent doesn't have time to make 1,000 phone calls and knock on 500 doors on the off chance that someone living there will want to buy or sell a house. If cold calling and door knocking were the only way to make it in real estate, I'd shut my doors immediately! I understand that desperate times call for desperate measures. But with the right business model, you'll never be that desperate.

Spamming

The mindset is this: If we are in your face long enough, eventually you'll pay attention. If you see my face on every email, billboard, postcard, park bench, and bulletin board, you'll remember me when you are ready to buy a house. Right? Wrong.

This kind of marketing doesn't work anymore. People HATE being bombarded with information that has little value, and they are immune to it. The public doesn't care about your 100 Percent Club status or that you earned your GRI designation. It doesn't matter if you send this type of information via email, snail mail, billboards, Facebook, or Twitter. It's annoying. They did not ask for this information, and they don't care about it. Stop sending it.

Always Be Closing

Traditional sales training tells you to "ABC Always Be Closing," and "Think positively, and you'll overcome all your cold calling fears," and "All you need to boost your sales is a few new sales techniques." But consumers detest salespeople, and they hate being 'sold' anything. Instead of a sales pitch, have a conversation. Instead of "closing," decide what is the right thing for your clients. Stop chasing every potential new lead. Stop trying to "overcome objectives." and try to find out the truth behind your client's concerns. Have real, meaningful conversations, and leave the cheap salesman tactics alone.

{ 4 }

Rose Bush, Brand New Agent

Real estate is like boot camp: only the strong survive. In fact, only about 12% stay in the business longer than 2 years. Why?

Let's Meet Rose

Let's walk in the shoes of Rose Bush. Rose is a woman in her early 40s. She graduated from a top university with above average grades and works for a local homebuilder. Day after day, Rose sits in an empty model home waiting for someone to come through the door and buy a house. She hates her boss and hates her life.

One day, Amway Realtor (AR) comes in with a buyer; she and Rose become friends. AR tells Rose all about her great company. They are well respected, offer full training, and even have profit sharing. She encourages Rose to explore her career options with this company.

Rose is a little turned off by the Amway tactics, but the thought of working as a real estate agent is intriguing; she wouldn't be trapped in a model home all day, and she could earn a lot more money. No weekly sales meetings. No miserable boss. It's a dream come true! She calls AR and asks her how to get started. First step, she's told, is to get her real estate license.

Real Estate School

Rose looks into real estate school and learns that each course is about $150; she only needs about six classes. Piece of cake! She excitedly signs up and hits the ground running.

The first class Rose takes is Real Estate Principles, the study of real estate related items you'll never need to know once you pass your licensing exam. The same is true for the rest of her courses: Real Estate Principles II, Contracts, Finance, Real Estate Law, and Ethics. She learns a lot of theory, but little practical information. That's okay, she thinks. Her broker will train her. AR said her broker is *famous* for their outstanding training! Rose completes her classes online and scores just high enough to pass the course. She's not worried about passing the licensing exam, however. She can spend $100 on the prep class and the school *guarantees* that she'll pass the test on the first try. As promised, she passes. Rose Bush is now qualified to work as a real estate agent. Hurray for Rose!

Rose Bush License #1,700,001 – Broker Shopping

Rose knows she has to find a broker to sponsor her before she can start to sell homes. No worries. She's already been approached by at least half a dozen brokers already.

She starts by visiting the broker of her good buddy, AR. They have a lot to offer: a good reputation, a beautiful office, and they will even teach her how to use her email program. Lots of online training courses are available, including time management, goal setting, how to handle objections, and how to show properties. The office in her neighborhood has about 300 agents! That's a good sign. They have Christmas parties, go out to lunch, and they were all very friendly when she took her tour of the office. It felt like a sisterhood and reminded her of her sorority days. Rose Bush + Amway Realtor = BFF. She really likes that this company is one of the largest growing companies in the nation. They have *thousands* of agents! She has to give up 40% of her commissions, but she's told that this is pretty standard since the broker gives her some leads. So far, it sounds pretty good!

Rose is no dummy, and she knows it is best to shop around for the right broker. Her next stop is to another large brokerage. This company has lots of sales incentives and awards their agents based on their sales volume. She likes the competitive spirit and the fact that she can keep 100% of her commission. They charge about $1,300/month in desk fees, but they don't accept new agents. Darn! They must be an elite group of Realtors, she says to herself. She'll get there – one day.

Rose decides to see what smaller, 100% commission brokerages are like and is curious about the $89/month desk fee. She learns that everyone works from home. They have training manuals that she can go through on her own time, and there is some broker support, but they have no profit sharing, no monthly lunches, and no Christmas party. She's responsible for her own website, insurance, stationary, and marketing. Rose is a people person. She sat alone in that model home long enough! She wants to be around other Realtors and make friends, and she decides that AR's broker might be the best fit for her. Rose is worried about the 40% commission split. That's a lot of money to give to your broker! But Amway Realtor reminds her that most agents in the office would happily pay 70% just for the privilege of working there! Over 300 (starving) agents can't be wrong! When she looks at it that way, 40% is a real bargain. Rose agrees and drinks the Kool-Aid.

Off She Goes!

Rose excitedly signs up with her new broker, but she isn't really prepared for all the expenses:

- NAR dues
- State dues
- Local board dues
- MLS fees
- Supra keys
- Supra deposit

And that's before she can even start to work! Next she needs:

- Business cards
- Yard signs
- Lock boxes
- Glamour shots
- "I Heart Referrals" Stickers

And don't forget:
- Website

- Flyers
- Postcards
- Other Realtor 'tools' she's told she needs

Rose is excited to attend her first company sales meeting. Dressed in her pencil skirt, pumps, and cubic zirconia Realtor pin, she feels all warm and fuzzy inside as the other agents in the office welcome her to the "team." They are all so nice, and the bagels were delicious (and free!). After a few of the agents discuss their new listings, the sales manager gives a very informative lecture about 'green' homes. "So much to learn," Rose says to herself. She decides she's glad she went with this broker. Each week they talk about different topics, like using Facebook and Twitter to market themselves. They even have a friendly competition to see who can generate the most revenue for the company. Mimosas on Thursdays, even! How fun!

Realizing that there is *so* much she doesn't know about real estate, Rose dives right into the company training manuals, starting with goal setting. Rose learns that once she puts her mind to it, *she can do anything!* She spends the next eight weeks taking classes and is happy that she has bonded with many of the other new agents in her office. They role-play, practice their listing presentations, and learn how to search for homes on the MLS. She learns about social networking, blogging, and lead generation. Feeling good!

Clients Wanted

Rose feels ready to take on her first client, if only she had one! She doesn't have a huge marketing budget, so she'll have to get creative. Feeling overwhelmed and anxious, she consults the "How to Be a Successful Real Estate Agent" guide on Wiki and goes through the steps. *The italicized parts are my thoughts.*

Step 1: Establish a mentoring relationship with a successful real estate salesperson.

Successful agents have no interest in training their competition. Sure, they might spend some time bragging to you about their success, and they might help you with the logistics while you are working with a client. You can count on a pep talk or two. But share the wealth? Don't count on it.

Step 2: Keep a database of all your contacts and make weekly contact with those who are looking for property services (buy, sell, lease, option).

No! If you want to keep your friends, stop spamming them with useless information! It's annoying and makes you look desperate.

Step 3: Do floor time. If you do not like "floor agent duty," then you probably are either already successful, or you will soon be run out of the business by those who do it.

Not all brokers allow newbies to do floor time. And a lot of agents find this to be a waste of time (although I have heard some success stories). Buyers and sellers shop for their agents online, they don't call their local real estate store, as if they were ordering a cake. Floor time might help you get a few leads, but it isn't a good long-term strategy. You're going to get sick of being your broker's receptionist.

Step 4: Look for innovative ways to make a splash in the local real estate market. *Yes, you need to do this. But how do you compete against 300 agents in your office who are all doing the same exact thing? What do you have to offer that's different? Special?*

Step 5: Use technology. Update your Twitter and Facebook statuses constantly so others will notice you are "into" real estate. Top of mind

awareness will grow. *Again, stop spamming people! Do you get spam from your CPA or Doctor? If you want to be treated like a professional, behave like one. If you want to be thought of as a cheap salesman, keep sending the spam.*

Step 6: Talk highly of other salespeople and brokers. *Why? You definitely shouldn't talk badly about other salespeople or brokers. But you shouldn't promote them either. And how will this help make Rose's phone ring?*

Step 7: Educate yourself with as many programs you can afford. *How many programs can you possibly need? Goal setting? How to motivate yourself? If your broker offers such great training, why do you have to look outside the brokerage for information?*

Step 8: Get listings. *Seriously?*

Step 9: Attend seminars. *Sitting in seminars won't make you any money! Realtors are sitting ducks for every Tom, Dick, & Harry who has something to sell, and most real estate seminars are sales presentations disguised as learning opportunities. You can't help a room full of Realtors buy a house, so what's the point?*

Step 10: Associate with successful agents. Don't get envious. Your mood will spill over to your customers! The end is near in that case. *Again, you can't sell another agent anything, so what's the point?*

Step 11: Become a broker in your state. The education alone will assist your knowledge base enough to provoke more success inducing

confidence. *The logic here is that she becomes a broker and then has the confidence in herself to be successful. Hmm.*

Step 12: Hold open houses. This is not for new agents only. You never know who will walk in; it could be your next listing client. *If open houses were an effective way to get listing leads, agents would hold their listings open themselves; they wouldn't allow another agent to do it. Open houses are, however, a good way to meet buyers. It's definitely a numbers game, and you might spend several hours bored stiff waiting for someone to walk through the door. If you have nothing better to do, and you lack a unique business model that has your phone ringing off the hook, it might be worth trying, but just like floor time, it's not a good long term strategy.*

Step 13: Read other situations and information from other veterans and educators. *Reading about other people's success won't help you be successful. Hard work will.*

Step 14: Use your time wisely. You have to prioritize your time for more important things. How you allocate your time is very important for your success. *Yes, spend your time on the things that will make you money. Sitting in sales meetings and attending seminars won't make you money. Goal setting won't make you money. Marketing something of value will.*

Rose quickly learns that this article is all fluff. What she needs is leads! She talks to her broker and to her AR mentor and is handed a couple of real estate motivational books. If she's willing to work hard enough, she'll be a success in no time. Make some cold calls! Knock on some doors! Visualize success! See it to believe it! Write it all down! Tape your goals to your mirror! If she's not successful, it's because she doesn't want to be!

Rose is pumped up! She wants to be a Realtor, and she's not going to give up. She goes online and compiles a list of ways to get real estate leads. Let's take a look:

- Referrals from satisfied customers
- Hang flyers or your card at the library, gym, grocery store, bars, etc.
- Online advertising (pay per click)
- Building relationships with business owners
- Creating a newsletter
- Getting involved in the community
- Sponsor a sports team
- Adopt a mile of highway to clean
- Join clubs
- Free sites like Craigslist
- Blog
- Build a website
- Spam forums
- Social networking
- Face-to-face networking
- Direct mail
- Know the right people
- Keep in touch with former clients
- Contact homeowner's associations
- Conduct free seminars
- Write e-zine articles
- Contact FSBO's
- Contact Expireds
- Send postcards to apartment complexes
- Send your farm area postcards once a month

- Wear your name tag
- Talk to people at the grocery
- Call 100 people a week
- Talk real estate in every conversation
- Pass out 40 business cards a week
- Door hangers

Some good ideas. Unfortunately, the other 80 new agents in her office have the same ideas and are selling the same services. Rose decides she'll have to do it better than everyone else, and she gets to work.

Rose's First Listing Appointment

Rose has been burning the midnight oil! She convinces a FSBO to let her stop by and talk about listing their home.

All dressed up and wearing her cubic zirconia encrusted pin in the shape of a house, Rose arrives right on time for her listing appointment. She looks good. She feels good. Her marketing materials are polished and professional.

After reading a quick paragraph from "Think and Grow Rich," she knocks on the door. The seller invites her inside, and Rose immediately notices a strange odor. And after looking around, she realizes that this house definitely needs some work! She tells the seller everything she'll do to sell their home quickly. She'll put it on the MLS so it'll be on Realtor.com, Zillow, Trulia, and all the other sites. She'll make a flyer and hold an open house. Rose is an honest person so she tells the seller that – based on its condition – the house should be priced at the mid to lower end of the price range. The seller doesn't like this at all! She shows him the seller's net sheet – again, he isn't happy! The seller tells Rose that a more experienced agent was there the day before, who said he could sell it for *a lot* more money. Rose is out! Oh well, she thought. At least she got some experience. Later, she'll play back the experience in her mind and meditate on how she can improve for next time.

Rose's First Buyer

Zillow's Premier Agent subscription paid off for Rose! A potential buyer calls and asks to see a home that is listed with her firm. Awesomeness! She believed it would happen, and it has. Rose makes plans to meet the buyer in an hour. Being the smart and cautious woman that she is, she gets the buyer's name and phone number and leaves it with the receptionist…just in case. Can't be too careful. Rose prints off the listing, grabs a few business cards and rushes out the door. The showing goes great! She really feels like she connected with the buyers, and they love the house. The buyers tell Rose they are going to have lunch and talk about things; they will get back to her with any questions. Rose is exhilarated and waits by the phone.

When she doesn't hear from them by the next morning, she gives them a call. No response. A few days and several calls and emails later, Rose finally reaches Mr. Buyer. Mr. Buyer thanks Rose for showing them the house. They want to buy it, but they have learned that they are entitled to their own representation. They've hired an Exclusive Buyer Agent to represent them. He'll keep her card, however, just in case. She reminds him that she can represent him as a "Buyer's Agent," but this buyer knows better. He wants proper representation, not smoke and mirrors. Rose is crushed. Isn't she the "procuring cause?" She should be paid for her efforts! Seeking comfort back at the office, she's told to hang in there. It's a numbers game, after all. If she's willing to work hard, she'll make it. If she's not successful, it's because she doesn't want to be. Rose decides to be proactive and knock on some doors. When nothing about her door knocking experience makes her feel better, she goes home and crawls into bed.

She's Outta Here!

Rose implements several more of the suggested marketing tactics and quickly blows through the money she set aside to launch her real estate career. Frustrated and feeling like a failure, Rose quits the business just like most new licensees before her.

It's Not Rose's Fault

What Rose and most new licensees don't know about real estate is a lot!! Here are some truths:

Brokering Real Estate Agents is Big Business

Owners of larger real estate firms stand to make a lot of money. There's nothing wrong with that; it's called capitalism. But the vast majority of agents never sell more than a few homes, if any. To stay in business, brokers *must* charge hefty desk fees and take a substantial cut of their agent's commissions. They draw agents into their web with promises of free training and an Amway-like business model. On the first day of training, agents are told to generate a list of everyone that they know – their "sphere of influence" – and call them weekly. Send them cookies and postcards. Drop by their home and office and ask the question, "Who do you know that wants to buy or sell a home?" The broker milks the agent's Rolodex, and their efforts, if successful, might result in a sale or two. But what happens after their friends and family stop answering their phone or opening the door?

At the end of the day, it's a numbers game. Brokers know that the majority of their agents are short-term players, so they get their money upfront and hope to generate a handful of superstar agents. The others are just their bread-and-butter agents that help keep the lights on. They recruit them, use them as lead sources, and when they fail, there are dozens more right behind them.

Educating Realtors is Big Business

There is big money involved with helping someone earn and maintain his or her license. There are also designations and credentials for sale, which allow the agent to feel a little more competitive, but serve no other useful purpose. There are motivational and training seminars and books like this one. It's not hard to spend thousands of dollars on courses and training you really don't need.

You Can't Count On Your Broker to Get You Leads

Leads are expensive. Brokers don't want to throw away leads on inexperienced agents, and on agents who don't care enough to do a good job. There was a time – 40 years ago – when you could count on your broker to generate enough leads to keep you in business. But things have changed. Brokers now take a 30-40% cut vs. a 50-60% cut. Brokers don't see lead generation as their job anymore. You have to generate your own leads or perish.

There are a TON of Hands in Your Pocket

There are companies selling software, hardware, ads, leads, supplies, websites, SEO, cars, insurance, billboards, books, training, designations, seminars, etc. It's quite easy for a new agent to get sucked into the "If I only had one more personalized pen, I'd be successful" mentality. And with *so many* fake promises, it's next to impossible to know which items are worth the money. This subject dominates most Facebook groups - which tools are worth it and which ones are wastes of money. Many, many agents have spent themselves out of the business by purchasing supplies that they don't need and that will never make them any money. For every person making a living as a Realtor, there are dozens making a living OFF of a Realtor.

Everyone is Doing the Same Exact Thing

Lead-generating companies are selling the same lead to multiple agents. For every listing appointment you have, there are three or four behind you who have more experience, a better sales pitch, or a lower price. It's very difficult to get noticed when so many agents are selling the same service, at the same price, to the same people, and in the same way.

It's a Tough Business

It's very difficult to succeed in real estate. In the next chapter, we'll talk about the #1 reason why agents like Rose are out of the business in less than two years.

{ 5 }

A Sea of Sameness

Rose's experience as a new Realtor is very, very common. The problem isn't that Rose is not capable, motivated, or qualified. The problem is that, in a sea of 1,700,000 Realtors, there are 1,699,999 other Realtors just like her! There is nothing unique about Rose or her skill set. There is nothing unique about her listing services. There is nothing unique about her buying services. There are 1,699,999 million Realtors doing the exact same thing as Rose.

It's a sad, sad sea of sameness.

Realtors are so scared of missing a lead that they try to keep themselves open to helping everyone. It can't be done. No one wants to stand out or be different, so they all dress the same, drive the same car, and market themselves in the same boring and ineffective way. Go to Realtor.com and take a look at the agent directory. Or visit some agent websites. Can you find anything unique or different about any of them?

The world doesn't need another generic Realtor.

To make it in this business over the long term, you need to be brave enough to buck the system. And you have to be able to brush off the negative feedback you will receive when you start to stand out. Other Realtors are not your friends. They are your competition, and their criticism (and advice) is to be taken with a grain of salt.

I don't understand why Realtors spend so much time "helping" each other succeed. Pepsi and Coke executives don't sit in the same boardrooms discussing the efficacy of their marketing campaigns. Why do Realtors?

One reason is that their brokers encourage it. In fact, they cater the event with bagels and gourmet coffee and mandate your participation. There is a psychology behind sales meetings. Dozens of books are written on how brokers can motivate their agents to sell more homes and how they can create a friendly competition. Don't share in these discussions. Just listen and learn from the smarty-pants agent who gets so caught up in being the Diamond Dog agent of the week that they share their best marketing secrets. Realtors love to brag about their success, even if their success is minimal. Let them spill the beans; you keep your mouth shut. Make friends with people who can send you business, like new home sales reps and loan officers. Don't befriend your competition.

Become a Specialist!

Any marketing expert will tell you that the secret to longevity in any business is to specialize. That's even truer in real estate where you have 1.7 million people chasing the same buyers and sellers.

Becoming a specialist allows you to define your target audience. Then, instead of being "Rose Bush, Same Realtor as the Lady in the Next Cubicle," you become "Rose Bush, Pink House Expert." Once you specialize, you can focus on your target market with sharp precision. It will be far cheaper and far more effective to structure your business this way.

Find Your Niche

It's not enough to become the expert in five zip codes or in four counties. That makes you the specialist of nothing. Later we will discuss what I know is the easiest and most rewarding way to make money in this business, but here are some other niche markets to consider:

- Luxury estates
- First-time buyers
- Condos
- Townhouses
- Distressed homeowners
- Historic properties
- Distressed properties
- Seniors
- Farms and ranches
- Commercial property
- Relocations
- Veterans
- Single moms
- Teachers
- Civil service
- Horse owners
- Investors

- Immigrants
- Downtown area
- Vacation property
- Golf course community
- Land
- Master-planned community

Once you've selected a target market, you can build your brand. All your marketing – your website, stationary, ads – can be focused on your niche. When you know whom your clients are, you'll know where to find them and how to reach them.

A Word of Caution

You can't "swing a dead cat" without finding a Realtor who specializes in something. While it's true that an agent who specializes in golf course communities, for example, will be far more successful than the agent who specializes in nothing, there is nothing inherently unique about it.

If you really want to make it, and make it big, you have to be willing to really put yourself out there. Be unique and let the stench of the industry roll off your back.

{ 6 }

Keys to Success

Once you have chosen a specialty, there are skills you must have in order to be successful. These skills are discussed next.

Lead Generation Skills

Most new agents fail because they don't know how to generate new business. If you can't generate new business, there is no way you are going to be successful. Period. If you're expecting your broker to provide you leads, you're in for a big surprise! Gone are the days when your broker would provide you with leads, marketing materials, and advertising. You might get a lead here and there from your broker, but if you're going to make it, you're going to have to make it on your own and generate your own leads.

What is it about lead generation that is so difficult? Is there something magical about Google Adwords? Do you have to have a marketing degree to place an ad in the paper or send out postcards to 5,000 people? Nope.

Here's the big secret to generating leads: You absolutely must be marketing a product or service that people will want and that 1.7 million other people aren't selling at the same time.

That's it! When you are offering a service that people want, that they can't get anywhere else, they'll be standing in line to work with you.

Technology Skills

Without computer skills, you will not be competitive. Others won't like working with you, and your days as a Realtor are numbered. While you certainly don't need to be a computer expert to have a career in real estate, at the very least you need to be proficient in:

- Email
- MLS (searching and inputting listings)
- Zipforms (contracts)
- Electronic signature software
- CMA software

Your local board will almost certainly offer classes in all of the above-mentioned programs. In Dallas, all these programs and more are included with monthly MLS fees, so there is nothing extra to buy. In addition, the board offers transaction management software, tax information, demographic information, and real estate statistics. While it's true that we all hate paying board fees, the products and services offered by the board in comparison to the money spent is the best bargain in town. If you haven't yet explored everything that your local board has to offer – at no additional cost – I highly recommend that you do so.

Supplies & Equipment

You need far less equipment than the Realtor vendors lead you to believe. You can get by with just the following:

- Computer, preferably a laptop
- Printer with scanning capability
- Supra key to enter homes
- Cell phone, preferably a smart phone
- Quality business cards
- Website

These items are the non-negotiables. There are plenty of sources for free contact management software, word processing, calendars, etc. Google Apps, for example, can keep you in business for years and years…and many apps are free! Don't overspend trying to get yourself "set up" to be a Realtor. You don't need fancy stationary or a service that allows you to create newsletters that no one reads. You don't need an Ipad AND a laptop AND a smart phone (although it's nice if you can afford it). Don't pay extra for the fancy CMA and Buyer Tour package when the basic package will work, at least for now. Be prudent with your money. Watch every penny. And out of every commission check set aside 25% for taxes and 25% for marketing. Make this a habit very early on in your career; you'll be glad you did.

The Right Broker

Choosing the right broker for you requires some introspection. Are you the corporate type or the freelance type? Do you need a lot of handholding? Are you self-motivated, or do you prefer a competitive environment? These days, there is a broker for everybody. Before you decide where to hang your license, there are some things you should know.

First, realize that real estate brokerage is big business! Between desk fees, overrides, and profits on supplies sold to their agents, brokers can stand to make a pretty penny! Their expenses, however, are sky high, so they need to recruit a lot of agents to cover their costs. How do they recruit so many agents? The promise of training.

Training is for suckers!

Training programs are used by brokerages as a recruiting tool. You don't need to take 100 classes to be a successful real estate agent; you just need a few of the right classes. You don't need to learn how to set goals; you need to provide a service that people actually want. Then it's easy to generate leads.

Brokers have been selling training to new agents for 50 years, and the vast majority of those new agents never see their second-year anniversary. That failure rate is criminal! But month after month, year after year, decade after decade, the beat goes on. Same sales pitch, same astronomical failure rate.

Does giving up 30 to 40% of your commission forever in exchange for training make sense to you? Why? You only need a few transactions under your belt to know what you're doing. To pay this kind of split over the long term is too high a price to pay. All new agents need training, but not nearly as much as you are led to believe. The promise of training is used by brokers to compete with other brokers in order to get agents to hang their licenses with them. Nothing else.

Let's talk about sales meetings. Sales meetings definitely serve a purpose. They promote competition among agents. Agents can update each other on their listings and possibly find an in-house buyer. Weekly achievements are recognized. Helpful? To some. But at what price?

What could you be doing to grow your business instead of spending your time in a sales meeting? Is it worth giving up 30 to 40% of your commission for the "privilege" of attending? Put another way, is it worth giving up $2,600 of your next $7,500 commission? How many bagels do you think you can buy for $2,600? Or better yet, how much advertising do you think you can do on your own for $2,600? A lot.

Choose the company with the best commission structure, lowest overhead costs, and best business model.

More About Brokers

I've done a little broker bashing, but I'm a broker and it's important that you understand the business from our perspective. Brokers invest a lot of time and a lot of money into new agents that never produce any income. Desk fees barely cover our expenses, and we spend months working with new agents only to have them quit the business to sell shoelaces on the Internet or go work as someone's assistant. There is a lot more deadwood in this business than there are superstars. We don't like to spend money generating leads, only to have them wasted by an inexperienced or apathetic agent. We'll spend hours helping you and training you, but the minute you mistreat a potential client, you're dead to us. That's the truth. There are no second chances.

Become an Expert

If you're going to specialize in historic properties, for example, make yourself an expert. Study historical architecture. Read everything you can about the materials used and the way people lived. Visit every historically significant home on the market, and understand how these homes were designed and constructed and why. There's a lot you can fake in real estate.

You can create an image by driving a fancy car and by wearing an expensive watch. You can glaze over the fact that you haven't yet completed your first transaction. You can get help writing contracts or running CMAs. But once you proclaim yourself to be an expert in historical properties, there's no faking it.

Risk Management

Like it or not, there is a certain amount of risk involved with being a Realtor; that's why we have Errors and Omissions insurance. But there is nothing worse than a Realtor who is so overly concerned about getting sued that they won't offer an opinion about anything.

It's true that we can't predict whether interest rates will rise or fall. But we can read financial reports and relay what we've read. We can say, "The Wall Street Journal predicts that interest rates will rise in the next 6 months. I tend to agree, but there is no way to know for sure." The agent who just says, "I can't speculate" is worthless and weak.

We can't guarantee the condition of the property, but we can provide an educated guess. You can say, "My best guess is that the roof is in good condition; your inspector will be able to tell us for sure."

We can't give legal advice, but we can explain the terms of the earnest money contract. Buyers and Sellers turn to Realtors for information; don't be afraid to give it to them. State your opinion and advise them where to turn for more information. But don't be a wimp. No one likes a person who is so concerned about covering their behind that they fail to do their job.

What You DON'T Need

We talked about the things you will need to succeed. The following are things people will try to sell you but that you really don't need to launch your career. You may want them. You may find value in them. But you can certainly get by without them.

Designations

The long string of letters we put next to our names is absolutely meaningless to the consumer. Let's get real. Earning your ABR, for example, is not like earning a CPA. A GRI is not an MD. Organizations make a lot of money off Realtors who are absolutely convinced that these designations matter. They really don't. You can tack on a long string of letters behind your name, and the only thing it really spells is SUCKER. The National Association of Realtors (NAR) unveils new designations all the time. Why? Follow the money. And agents lap it up like crazy. In a desperate attempt to one up the guy in the next cubicle, agents are first in line to sign up for the latest and greatest Accredited Sales Strategy (ASS) designation. Credentials are for sale and anyone can buy them. They will drain your bank account but will do very little else, except maybe make you feel a little more competitive. Here is a list of some of the designations and certifications available for Realtors just from the NAR:

- Accredited Buyer's Representative (ABR)
- Accredited Land Consultant (ALC)
- Certified Commercial Investment Member (CCIM)
- Certified International Property Specialist (CIPS)
- Certified Property Manager (CPM)
- Certified Real Estate Broker (CRB)
- Certified Residential Specialist (CRS)
- Counselor of Real Estate (CRE)
- General Accredited Appraiser (GAA)
- NAR's Green Designation (GREEN)

- Graduate, Realtor Institute (GRI)
- Performance Management Network (PMN)
- Realtor Association Certified Executive (RCE)
- Residential Accredited Appraiser (RAA)
- Society of Industrial and Office Realtors (SIOR)
- Seniors Real Estate Specialists (SRES)
- At Home With Diversity (AHWD)
- Broker Price Opinion Resource (BPOR)
- NAR's E Pro (e PRO)
- Military Relocation Professional (MRP)
- Resort & Second Home Property Specialist (RSPS)
- Short Sales & Foreclosure Resource (SFR)

Madness. And according to a recent survey (discussed later), less than 1% of consumers select an agent based on their designations. If you can get a designation at the same time that you're taking your continuing education classes, great. If you decide to specialize in the senior market, the senior designation makes sense. If you work only with buyers, the ABR might be a good idea. But don't overvalue these designations. They aren't that important.

Search Engine Optimization

There are a gazillion real estate related websites online! Yes, your website needs to be optimized so that Google and other search engines can find you, but the chances of your new website ending up number one in an organic search are pretty small. You can spend five thousands dollars trying to make it happen, but someone else is going to spend ten thousand. Fight the fights you can win; this isn't one of them.

Things That Help You Spam

Stop spamming people! No more newsletters written by a ghost writer, no more emails with gardening tips, no more "Don't Keep Me a Secret" post-cards, no cold calls, no door hangers, no door knocking, no more Amway tactics to recruit agents into your firm. Stop! Stop being Mr. or Mrs. Spam Guy and start being Mr. or Mrs. Well-Respected Professional. If you have systems in place to attract people to your unique business model, you won't have to behave like an ambulance chasing attorney.

Video Equipment & Cameras

High-quality virtual tours and listing photos are critical, I agree. But I know agents who take pictures and videos with their smartphone, and the level of quality that they produce is acceptable for most of their listings. Homes without a lot of natural light or high-end luxury homes might require a higher-quality photograph. But, for the most part, it's hard to justify the cost of expensive equipment, especially early on in your career. There are services that can do this for you better and cheaper. Don't spend money in anticipation of future business. If and when you get a listing, hire someone to photograph the house for you if you're not able to do a good job on your own. Save your money for your marketing campaigns.

Educational Seminars

Early in my career, I attended every free real estate related seminar I could find. In fact, I learned about Exclusive Buyer Agency when a speaker selling a lead generation program mentioned in passing the new trend of exclusive buyer's agency that was starting in California. I was the only one in a room of about 300 people who picked up on it, apparently, because my company was the only Exclusive Buyer's Agency in Dallas for several years. Going to seminars can be motivational, inspirational, and you can learn a few things. I still listen to a webinar on occasion. But think hard before you spend your money this way, and remember that you're not going to make any money sitting around in a seminar.

Lead-Generating Programs

I would LOVE, LOVE, LOVE to be able to pay an online marketing company X dollars a month and receive a steady stream of highly qualified leads. It wouldn't even matter that 90% of the leads are junk! I can earn a living on the other 10%. I would sign up with every marketing company in the country if it were that easy.

It doesn't work this way. Most of these services are simply placing pay per click ads on the various search engines and selling the leads to you (and many other agents) at triple the price you would pay if you placed the ad yourself. You don't need them to do that for you; it's a very simple process. And lead-generating companies that charge you 'per click' are riddled with fraudulent tactics to artificially pad your bill. If you're going to buy leads, be sure to have tracking software on your website so you can audit your lead source. Google Analytics offers a great way to keep track of how many people are visiting your site. The service and code is all free.

Online marketing should definitely be part of your marketing plan, but be very careful about the services you buy. Check the BBB and Ripoff Report, and ask for feedback from other Realtors. Remember to take the advice of other Realtors with a grain of salt since they are your competition and don't necessarily want you to succeed. You should also know that marketing companies put trolls on sites like Active Rain to promote their services. Do your research, and don't make long-term commitments. Two or three months is plenty of time to determine if the service will work for you.

{ 7 }

Flat-Fee Exclusive Buyer Agency

I've been teasing you throughout the book about an easier way to earn a great living as a real estate agent. Well, here it is: Flat-Fee Exclusive Buyer Agency.

Exclusive Buyer's Agency

Let's face it. In a real estate transaction, the buyer assumes all of the risk. The seller walks away from the property and is free of any obligation or responsibility. The buyer pays for inspections, appraisals, closing costs, and ends up with the house and a mortgage. At best, buying a home is a complicated process. At worst, it can be an emotional and financial nightmare. Not only do buyers have to find a house that they love, they have to verify its condition, negotiate a good price, figure out how to pay for it, insure it, move in, all the while ensuring they are buying a home that they will be able to resell for a profit when the time comes. The list of things to consider is seemingly endless.

Before 1989, all real estate agents worked for the seller and these agents were not required to disclose this fact to the buyer. The agent would spend many days in the car with a potential buyer, and that buyer had no idea that the agent had a fiduciary duty to tell the seller everything the buyer said. If the buyer offered $400,000 for a house, but stated that they would be willing to go up to $450,000, the agent was required by law to pass that information along to the seller.

As expected, lawsuits were filed across the country when buyers learned that they could have purchased property for a lot less money had they known whom the agent represented. As a result, most states implemented disclosure requirements. At the first meeting with a potential buyer or seller, agents were required to disclose to the buyer which party they represented. Most states implemented policies and procedures that gave the illusion of fairness, but one thing remains the same: The buyer still assumes the risk and the buyer is still the target of most of the fraud.

In a perfect world, the buyer and seller would each pay their own agent. Dual agency wouldn't exist, and loan fees would be fixed. But it will never work that way. Why? Buyers need cash for their down payment and closing costs. Homeownership would be out of reach for a tremendous number of homebuyers if we asked them to pay their agent's commission in addition to the other expenses they incur when buying a home. Rolling commissions into the transaction and paying the agents out of the seller's proceeds makes buying and selling a home possible. It's that simple.

See the Light

When you're ready to step away from the herd and make a steady, stable, bountiful income in real estate, working as an Exclusive Buyer Agent is the way to go. Exclusive Buyer Agents (EBA) represent homebuyers ONLY. They work for companies that never take listings and never represent sellers. This eliminates the conflict of interest that exists when one company tries to represent both the buyer and the seller at the same time.

Exclusive Buyer Agency is a specialty that is in demand and is endorsed by Suze Orman, Ralph Nader, Kiplinger's, HUD, Business Week, the New York Times, and many, many more. EBAs offer buyers the highest level of consumer protection available. A lot of people – even Realtors – confuse "Buyer Agents" with "Exclusive Buyer Agents." Buyer Agents work with buyers one day and sellers the next. Their broker represents buyers and sellers. EBAs work for companies that never, ever, ever take listings or represent sellers. There is never a conflict of interest that will jeopardize the buyer's negotiating position.

Little to No Competition

Less than ½ of 1% of Realtors work as Exclusive Buyer Agents. Why? For one, as we discussed earlier, some agents don't like the idea of limiting their business to just buyers. They are so afraid of losing a lead that they try to be a jack-of-all-trades rather than become an expert in one specific area.

Is it smart to give up working with sellers? It's brilliant, actually. When you stop competing with the thousands of seller agents in your area, you become your city's "go to" person for buying a home. When people want to buy a house without getting ripped off, they'll call you.

Another reason fewer agents work strictly with buyers is that working with buyers is often more work than working with sellers (except the way I do it). Buyer agents drive their clients around and look at dozens of homes. They write contracts, negotiate the deal, help with home inspections, financing, and hold the buyer's hand all the way through closing. It's a lot of work, and there's no guarantee of a paycheck.

Lastly, and as I mentioned earlier, most Realtors are sheep that travel in herds. They don't like to buck the system or be unique. They want to work for a company that is "kind of, sort of like a corporation, but not really." They say they want to be an entrepreneur, but either don't have the skills or are not fully committed. They want to be affiliated with a name because they think it gives them credibility, even though it really doesn't. They will toe the line, even if it means their real estate career is a miserable failure.

Feel Great About Your Job

Exclusive Buyer Agents are typically terrible sales people. They don't feel comfortable with the traditional, aggressive sales tactics used by most real estate agents. EBAs are caretakers and are genuinely concerned about the welfare of their buyer/clients. Yes, they want to earn a nice living, but they don't sacrifice our clients for the benefit of a paycheck. They are consumer advocates...the boy scouts/girl scouts of real estate.

In 2011, the National Association of Realtors asked consumers, "What are the most important factors when choosing an agent?"

Here are the results:

31% - Agent is honest and trustworthy

23% - Reputation of agent

16% - Agent is a friend or family member

11% - Agent's knowledge of the area

10% - Agent has caring personality

3% - Agent's association with a certain firm

1% - Professional designations

4% - Other

The biggest concern for the consumer is the agent's perceived trustwor-thiness. Dedicating yourself to the protection and representation of only homebuyers goes a long way in validating your integrity, especially when you couple Exclusive Buyer Agency with the pricing model discussed next.

Flat-Fee vs. Traditional Pricing

My company offers both flat-fee and traditional pricing. Traditional pric-ing is the customary (but negotiable) 3% commission that is paid out of the seller's proceeds at closing. The seller agrees to pay a 5 to 7% commission to the listing agent, and the listing agent agrees to share the commission with the agent who brings the buyer. It's the system that has been in place for dec-ades.

Flat-fee pricing is a brand-new concept in the world of buyer agency and what I believe will become more and more commonplace in the future. Flat-fee pricing means the agent's commission stays the same regardless of the sales price. I earn the same commission if I sell a $200,000 house as if I sell a $250,000 house. It's fair and honest, and it's in line with the philosophies of Exclusive Buyer Agency and consumer advocacy.

Truth be told, it's no more work to help someone buy a $200,000 home than it is a $300,000 home. The buying process is the same. It may take a little longer to tour the property, but everything else is an equal amount of work.

Flat-fee pricing eliminates integrity battles. If the Realtor earns more money when the buyer pays a higher price, how can the buyer really trust them to negotiate the lowest price on their behalf? Because they have a signed Buyer's Rep Agreement? Because they have a fiduciary duty towards the buyer? Nope. The concept is counterintuitive. It's unfair to ask the buyer to trust us with such an important transaction when they have no concrete reason to do so. It's just too large a leap of faith. Flat-fee pricing takes the issue off the table. When my commission stays the same regardless of the sales price of the home, the buyer knows for certain that I'm not trying to get them to spend more money just so I can pad my commission.

Flat-fee pricing means limited service.

Am I willing to show buyers 30 to 40 homes for months on end for a reduced commission? Absolutely not! I'm a businessperson and time is money; I don't discount my commission for anyone.

Today's buyers start their home search online. They can scout neighborhoods, do preliminary research, and easily narrow their list down to 12 houses.

Flat-fee pricing means this: I will work for a flat rate of $XXX, if the following conditions are met:

1. I only have to show them 12 houses or less
2. I make less than 3 trips to show them homes (I don't want to show them 12 houses, one at a time)
3. They come to me with a recent pre-approval letter
4. They are ready, willing, and able to buy within 60 days
5. They pay my deposit

When these conditions are met, I will be paid my flat fee and the remaining commission will be rebated to the buyer at closing.

Flat-fee pricing is NOT discounting!

"Discounting" is doing the same amount of work for a lower price. "Flat-fee pricing" is doing less work for less money. It's allowing the buyer to share in the commission in exchange for doing the legwork. If you want to make a stable, steady, substantial income, flat-fee exclusive buyer agency is the way to go.

Benefits of Flat-Fee Pricing

Flat-fee pricing pays the buyer to do the vast majority of the shopping. It keeps them out of your car and eliminates you having to show them dozens of homes over a 3- or 4-month period of time. Showing fewer homes means you have more time to work with other buyers or more time to spend with your family. Working with more buyers means you can scale your business without hiring a team of agents to work with you.

The shared commission keeps the buyer loyal to you. They are not going to work with another Realtor after they have partnered with you and are getting cash back at closing. Why would they? Not only are they getting the highest level of buyer representation available, they are getting a rebate at closing. It's a pretty good deal for you and for them.

Flat-fee pricing stabilizes your income because it's pretty darn easy to find clients. Would you rather have $10,000 in commissions each and every month, or $5,000 one month, $0 the next, and $15,000 the next? I want a paycheck every single month. I want easy, grateful buyers and fast closings. I don't want to be a tour guide or spend hours on end with buyers and hope that they buy something through me. If I can offload the 'grunt' work to the buyer, I'm more than happy to share my commission with them. I can work with three buyers in the time it takes most agents to get one to the closing table. My value is not in searching the MLS for homes; any monkey can do that. My value is in what comes after the buyer finds a property they wish to purchase. If buyers are willing to free up my time so that I can do more of the important work, I'm happy to reward them with a rebate.

When you become one of the few Exclusive Buyer Agents in your area, and the only EBA that offers flat-fee pricing, finding buyers is easy. You have something unique to offer. When people want to buy a home without getting ripped off, they'll come to you. When they want to buy a house, but only need to look at a few homes, they'll come to you. You'll have a steady stream of clients who remain loyal to you. They'll tell their friends. Before long, you won't have to do any marketing at all.

And Now, The Downside

Yes, there is a downside to working this way, but the list of positives far exceeds the list of negatives.

Leaving Money on the Table

It's not always an easy thing to rebate $10,000, for example, back to the buyer at closing. Believe me, I know! But if you're going to market yourself as flat fee, you have to abide by the terms of your agreement. The good news is that most flat-fee buyers look at very few homes before they pull the trigger, and you are being paid very, very well considering the small amount of time you spend with them. Also, these are buyers you probably wouldn't have if you were working as a traditional agent. Buyers (especially higher-end buyers) LOVE the flat-fee pricing model and take comfort in knowing they are getting the highest level of buyer representation available anywhere. Don't worry about the individual paychecks. It doesn't matter what you earn a month; it matters what you earn in a year. When you see what you've earned at the end of the year, I know you'll be very, very happy. And remember that if the buyer can't meet the requirements of the flat-fee pricing program, they automatically convert to the traditional full-service program.

Other Realtors Will Discourage You

The other downside to working as a flat-fee Exclusive Buyer Agent is the misconception by other Realtors that you're a "discounter." Say the word "discounter" in a room full of Realtors and watch what happens! Swords are drawn, fists fly, and the room is soon littered with "Welcome Home" buttons. Realtors don't like to compete on price. I don't blame them. Competing on price is a good way to lose in this rat race.

Again, flat-fee pricing is not discounting. Discounting is doing the same job for less money. My flat-fee program is less work for less money. There's a big difference.

Most of the time, the seller's side has no knowledge of the arrangement you have made with your buyer. All they see is the 3% commission on the closing statement. It's nobody's business how much you keep and how much you give away. Learn to let the chatter roll of your back. Ignore the people that tell you you're heading down the wrong path because chances are they are making $25,000 a year, if that.

Combining Flat-Fee And Traditional Pricing

The level of service involved with flat-fee pricing is not sufficient for every buyer. First-time homebuyers and buyers relocating from a different state, for example, don't always like the confines of the flat-fee model. For these buyers, I work for 3% of the sales price paid out of the seller's proceeds at closing, like any traditional agent. Some of my buyers start out as flat-fee clients but later realize they need more help. They may back out of a contract, change areas, or can't make a decision after seeing just 12 houses.

Anything that falls out of my stated requirements for flat-fee pricing automatically converts to traditional pricing, discussed later in this chapter.

The only exception I make is when a buyer looks at 13 houses instead of the maximum of 12, for example. I'm not going to be a jerk and deny the buyer their rebate simply because they looked at one extra house. At the same time, my services aren't free. I will add a little extra to my fee to cover my time and expenses when this happens, usually an extra $200 per showing, but it varies based on the location and whether or not I have to make an extra trip.

Exclusions

Certain transactions should be completely excluded from your flat-fee pricing program:

- Short Sales
- Foreclosures
- Building a home
- FSBOs
- Investment Property

All of the above require FAR too much work to qualify for flat-fee pricing. Remember, you don't want to do the work of a traditional agent for a reduced rate. That's discounting. Reduced fee means reduced service.

Never Do the Following!

One of the complaints listing agents have about discounters is that the discount agent doesn't carry their weight. The listing agent gets stuck doing the job of the buyer's agent. This is never, ever okay!

Flat-fee pricing is not discounting! Have I made this point clear?

When you limit your service, you are only limiting the number of homes you show. You are still responsible for all the other tasks that a buyer agent normally performs.

Here's another thing that is not okay. There is a large, discount Internet broker who advises their buyers to have the listing agent show them a house, and then contact them if they want to make an offer. More often than not, the Internet broker never even sees the house. Because the listing agents are professionals, they will accommodate and show the house, but most of the time they have no idea that this buyer is represented elsewhere. The listing agent ends up doing more than their fair share of the work, and the Internet broker is unfairly compensated for work they don't do.

It's your job to view homes with your buyers.

On occasion, I get a buyer who looks at homes with the listing agent so they can stay within their 12 showing limit. They want to view their short list of homes with me so that I can advise them. I release buyers who go behind my back and abuse the listing agents this way. If they want to look at more than 12 homes, that's fine. They can convert to the full-service program or pay me per house. And if my buyer wants to buy a house that was shown to them by the listing agent, I always make sure that he or she is compensated properly for their time at closing (out of the buyer's proceeds, of course). Technically, it's the listing agent's job to weed out these types of buyers, but most want to represent their seller properly, so they take a chance and show the house. I respect that.

Know Your Stuff!

Exclusive Buyer Agents have a higher level of care and duty than suba-gents or regular buyer agents. If you are going to call yourself a home buying expert, you better know what you're talking about! You need to know how to:

- Analyze floor plans
- Determine property values
- Spot defects in a property
- Write a contract that protects your buyer
- Protect your buyer from predatory lenders
- Much, much more

In the chapters ahead, I'm going to teach you what you need to know to represent a homebuyer properly. You will still have some work to do, how-ever. Real estate laws vary by state, as do contracts and processes. And it's one thing to read about foundation issues; it's another thing to see it in per-son. I strongly recommend that you find an inspector who will let you tag along to an inspection or two. Meet a few loan officers and visit a couple of title companies. The best training doesn't happen online or in a book. Get out there! Make some friends and see things live, in action, with your own two eyes. Believe me, it's time well spent.

{ 8 }

Working With Buyers

Exclusive Buyer Agents act as consumer advocates, not as sales people. But we're good friends and parents, and are very service-oriented. As you go through the following pages, imagine you're helping your little brother or sister buy a home. Your buyers look to you for help, comfort, and guidance; it's an honor that they put their trust in you! Take them under your wing and lead them through the complicated and intimidating process of buying a home.

Lead Generation

It would be absurd for me to publish my marketing materials and to tell you how I generate my leads. I have agents that work for me, and they are the only ones privy to much of that information. But generating leads when you have a business model like mine isn't hard. Here are some general tips.

Since 80% of buyers begin their search online, the bulk of your marketing efforts should start there. Your ads should be very targeted and area specific. Google Adwords, Facebook Ads, Google +, Yahoo Business, and Bing are good places to start, if you have the budget. Build a website that talks about your services but don't even try to compete with the big players like Realtor.com, Zillow, or Trulia. All you need is a clean, informative, professional website. No one will use your fancy financial calculators, and they won't read about 80% of what's on your site. Go for clean, simple, and professional. It's far better to have a beautiful four-page website than it is to have a messy, "home grown" site that is difficult to navigate. Keep it simple.

Most of the lead-generation services (Market Leader, Trulia, Zillow) are geared towards listing agents, but with a little creativity you can make it work for you. Reviews are mixed on the efficacy of these sites, so proceed with caution. Postcards and press releases have produced some results for me, as has an ad in my local, small town paper. Think about who might be buying a home and then learn how to find them.

In previous chapters, I included lots and lots of lead-generating tips. When used by the everyday agent, most of them don't work because they have nothing unique to offer. The opposite is true when you're an Exclusive Buyer Agent. We stand out and get noticed. You'll find it much, much easier to generate leads using this business model.

First Contact

Buyers will contact you for the first time via email or by phone. Remember that you're not going to be able to work with everyone who calls you. Don't be so desperate for your first sale that you forget to weed out the time wasters and the buyers who aren't ready, willing, and able to buy a house. Your goals for your first contact are discussed in the following sections.

Decide if You Can Help Them

Don't waste your time or theirs if you can't help them. Where do they want to buy a home? Do you work that area? When do they need to move? If they are buying a home six months from now, you should still meet with them and solidify the relationship, but you don't want to start showing houses until they are ready, willing, and able to buy. You have other clients who need your attention (or you will).

Explain Exclusive Buyer's Agency and Your Pricing Policy

Assuming these are buyers you can help, talk to them about your unique service offerings. Explain full service vs. flat-fee pricing. If they require full service representation, be sure you have time to accommodate them. Explain why it's so important to have exclusive buyer representation vs. a regular buyer agent. To recap, a regular buyer agent is really just a dual agent in disguise. One day they work for the seller, the next for the buyer. Exclusive Buyer Agency means buyers only. Here's a story that I often tell my prospective clients to explain the difference between an Exclusive Buyer Agent and a Buyer Agent.

> *"Suppose you drive by a house that interests you and notice that there is a Century 21 sign in the yard. You decide to call the number printed on the sign, and a very nice Realtor answers the call. This Realtor was hired by the owners of the house to sell their property and get them as much money as possible.*
>
> *On the phone, the Realtor offers to show you the house, so you set up a time to meet and view their listing. You like the house, but*

are not ready to commit, so the Realtor offers to show you some other homes that you might like.

While looking at the first house, the Realtor represented the seller. Now they've showing you other agent's listings in which they would represent you as a buyer's agent, should you opt to buy one of those homes.

In the meantime, they have asked you all kinds of questions and have a clear picture of your purchasing power and the level of your motivation. If you decide to buy the first house they showed you (or any of their other listings), they would have to turn you over to someone else in their office, but would be legally obligated to tell their seller/client everything they know about you. And, from the seller's standpoint, the agent used their house as a source of buyer leads. The seller most likely shared all of their secrets with this agent, only to have that information used against them if both the buyer side and seller side of the transaction are handled in house with the same broker. It's a convoluted mess, and it is unfair to both the seller and the buyer, and the only person who wins here is the Realtor and their broker."

The point is not to make a listing agent seem like a bad guy, but to help the buyer understand how the laws of agency affect them. These laws exist for a reason. It matters who represent them.

Offer a Free Home Finder Account

Most MLS services include the ability to have new listings sent to your clients automatically; I call this service Home Finder. In Texas, buyers have their own 'portal' and can sort through listings, take virtual tours, ask their agent questions, and more. Buyers love it. If this service is available in your area, set up an account for your prospect or client. If not, offer to send them a list of homes that may suit their needs.

Ask them if they have seen anything they like

More often than not, buyers have come across a few homes online that interest them. Ask them to send you the addresses of the homes they like so that you can check their status, and so that you can learn their taste and preferences. It will give you things to talk about with them later.

Set Up a Time for a Strategy Session

Your last order of business is to set up a time to meet. I call it a strategy session, but it's really an opportunity for you and the buyer to decide if you like each other. Do not hang up without getting the following information:

- Name, phone number, home address
- Email address
- Spouse's name and email address
- Places of employment

You need this information to confirm their identity in advance of your first meeting. Go online and see what you can learn about your buyers. All you're really trying to do is to confirm that they are who they say they are for security reasons, but you'd be surprised what you can learn about them by looking at their LinkedIn or Facebook pages. The more you know is a good idea.

Safety First – Always

First meetings with buyers should always be held at a public place like Starbucks or your office. It's NEVER a good idea to meet a buyer for the first time at an empty house. Always let a family member or friend know where you will be and whom you will be meeting. Don't ignore the issue of safety! There are a lot of nut jobs out there, and Realtors are easy targets. Follow your instincts. If you get a vibe that you are not safe, don't work with them. Eventually, you'll be alone in a house with them and will be in an extremely vulnerable position. There will be other clients; I promise.

Strategy Session

Lots of buyers are tempted to skip the strategy session and move right into looking at homes. This is a bad idea for a number of reasons. First, it's not safe to meet strangers in empty homes. We already discussed this. Second, you need to explain to your buyers their responsibilities in the flat-fee program vs. the full-service program. Be sure you want to spend the next month or two working with them. You're going to have your pick of clients; pick ones you like. And, lastly, you only want the buyers who are ready, willing, and able to buy. Until you have a paycheck in hand, you are working as a volunteer. There are dozens of desperate agents who will drop everything to show a house; these are the agents that get used and abused by buyers. Your buyers need to be respectful of you and your time. If they insist on viewing a few homes, that's perfectly fine. But these showings count toward their 12 showing maximum, if they are flat-fee clients. Meet them at a public place first, conduct your strategy session, and then go look at the homes. If you don't, you'll end up working for free. Don't behave like a full-service, traditional agent and then give them back part of your commission. We earn a limited commission because we provide a limited service.

Assessing Buyer's Needs

Hopefully you learned a great deal about the buyer on the phone or through your email communications. Use the first few moments of your time together to build rapport and 'make nice.' They may start asking you questions right away, or they may want you to take the lead. Many first-time homebuyers learn about the homebuying process through books, like Home Buying for Dummies, Nolo's Essential Guide to Buying a Home, or my book, Buying a Home: Don't Let Them Make a Monkey Out of You! You should be prepared to answer the questions provided in these books for buyers and explain how you will work together to meet their needs. The following sections include discussion topics to ensure you have identified all their housing needs.

Number of bedrooms and bathrooms

In terms of resale, the safest size single-family home is a four bedroom. Anyone who can fit into a three-bedroom home would fit into a four-bedroom home. The opposite is not true. A family who needs a four-bedroom home would never consider a three-bedroom home. Three bedrooms are perfectly fine if a nice selection of four-bedroom homes is not available in their price range. But, if they do buy a three-bedroom home, it is a nice bonus to have at least two living areas in the house or a space for an office.

Single-Story or Two-Story

There are both advantages and disadvantages to either a single-story or a two-story home. In a single-story home, the ceilings can be higher, and there is no noise from people walking overhead. It is easier and safer for small children and the elderly or disabled to live on one floor, and there is no wasted space where the stairs would go. On the down side, the yard is usually smaller due to the larger footprint of the house. There is typically less privacy, and the bedrooms are often smaller.

Living in a two-story home usually means nice views from the second floor and more separation between living spaces and bedrooms. It's safe to leave windows open on the second floor, the yard is sometimes larger, and if all the bedrooms are upstairs, the first floor doesn't have to be heated or cooled at night (assuming you have zoned heat/air). The negatives are the noise level when people are walking on the second floor, and that stairs can be inconvenient and prohibitive if a family member becomes injured or sick.

Number of living areas

Most of my clients are very happy not to have a formal living area, opting instead for a home office. The family room is typically where everyone gathers, so make sure this space is on the larger side, and be mindful of traffic patterns once all the furniture is in place. You typically need a 3' wide walkway to move from space to space. If your clients have children and want them to have a separate space for their toys and friends, be sure to find a home with at least two living areas. Many people like to have a separate game room just for the kids and their mess.

Number of dining areas

Although people don't often use their formal living space anymore, there is still a strong demand for a formal dining room; it is preferable to have a minimum of two eating areas. Since most meals will be in the breakfast room, it is important that this space be large enough to accommodate a table and at least four chairs comfortably. If the door to the back yard is in the breakfast room, be sure that there will be room to open the door once the dinette is in place. The dining room should accommodate a minimum of six people. The only exception to this rule applies to townhomes where a single eating area is somewhat common.

Garage spaces

In most parts of the country, single-family homes usually come with a two-car garage. You may encounter homes where the homeowners have converted the garage into living space. Be sure that the space can be converted back to a garage easily, since homes without garages are harder to sell. If they are purchasing a home in a neighborhood where most of the homes have a three-car garage, they shouldn't buy a home with a two-car garage. You want your buyer's house to blend with the other homes in the neighborhood.

Square Feet

It's smart to have a general idea of what 3000 square feet, for example, looks and feels like, but do not get too concerned about numbers. The floor plan matters more than the square footage of the house. A good floor plan can make a 2500 square foot home feel like a palace. Conversely, a 4000 square foot home can feel small if there is not enough usable space or if the design is poor. If your buyers think they want a 3000 square foot home, show them homes in the 2700 to 3300 square foot range. You never know when a house they look at will be THE house, even though it wasn't perfect on paper.

Age of home

If your buyers are concerned about energy conservation and utility bills, newer is better by far. The cost to cool a home built in the 1980s can be triple the cost to cool the same size home built in the year 2000 or later. Improvements in the quality of insulation, windows, roof decking/radiant barriers, energy star appliances, and air conditioners have substantially reduced the costs to heat and cool a home. Sacrifices are to be made, however. Older homes were typically built on bigger and sometimes more beautiful lots, and have a much different look and feel than new homes, for better or for worse. If your buyers are not sure of their preference, show them a few older homes. They will know right away if older homes are something they wish to consider.

Area

Help your buyers decide where they want to live. How far are they willing to drive to get to work? Do they want to be close to downtown or are they happy in the suburbs? Schools are always an important consideration, and they should buy a home in a good school district, even if they don't have children. An afternoon in the car can answer a lot of their questions. Note that driving around the different areas is something they can do on their own, unless you're taking them on as full-service clients.

Yard Size

A large yard generally means more maintenance. If your buyers are not willing to do the work themselves, they should make sure they have the money to hire someone to take care of it for them. Generally speaking, people like a larger yard. Unless they are buying a townhouse, they shouldn't buy a house with the smallest yard in the neighborhood, because they may have a hard time selling the property later. Play the averages and find a home that has an average size lot or bigger.

Price range

There is a big difference between how much money the bank will lend buyers and how much they can truly afford. Just because the bank will lend them $400,000, doesn't mean they should borrow that much. Have them consider the monthly cost of utilities, repairs, cleaning, maintenance, and furniture. Bankrate.com has some great mortgage calculators to help them decide how much home they can comfortably afford. Buyers should aim to buy everything they need, but just some of the things they want. There is a difference.

Property Condition

How much work are they willing to do? They might be open to making cosmetic changes like paint, carpet, etc., but it is important to know their limits. If they are going to make changes to the property before they move in, be sure they have the money for both labor and materials, even if they plan to do the work themselves. They need to have some "oops" money set aside.

Pool

People don't always realize the work and money involved with maintaining a pool. The costs include heating, cleaning, chemicals, and insurance, and there is the constant concern about the safety of your children, pets, and even the neighborhood children. If they are not 100 percent certain that they want a pool, they shouldn't get one. However, if they know for certain that they do want one, it is much smarter to buy a home with a pool already installed. If they add a pool later, it is likely they will only recuperate about 50 percent of their original cost, at best, when they decide to sell the home.

How to Read MLS Listings

In my area, the "Full Agent Report" contains the private remarks that listing agents share with other agents. When you're representing buyers, it's your job to share this information. Always print out a listing and teach them how to read it. Buyers are always interested in days on market, cumulative days on market, price per square foot, which level the rooms are on, the number of living areas, and the lot size.

Buyer's Representation Agreement

In my opinion, buyer's representation agreements are worthless. Why? They aren't really enforceable, and the only real purpose they serve is to intimidate the buyer and discourage them from being disloyal to you. The purpose of a buyer's rep agreement should be to clarify expectations. That's it. My agreement is written more like a disclosure.

- There is no beginning and end date; the buyer is free to walk away at any time (so am I, by the way).
- I describe in detail how I will be paid and by whom.
- My deposit is explained (discussed later).
- I disclose my agency relationship (all buyers, all the time).

I don't even care if the buyer signs it since, in Texas, the buyer can authorize me to represent them verbally. Buying a home is the biggest and most important purchase in most people's lives. Why make it more scary and stressful when it's not necessary to do so? Working with you should be the least scary part of their experience. I know a buyer is serious about working with me when they show up with their checkbook to leave me a deposit.

Am I going to sue them if I show them a house on Monday and they buy a house through a builder on Tuesday? Of course not. While it's true that with the proper buyer's representation agreement I could take them to court and be awarded damages to collect my commission, chances are I would never collect a dime, so why bother? I can work with 10 other buyers in the time it takes to sue one. It's very, very rare that I have a buyer who is disloyal to me, but if I do, it's my fault for not ensuring their confidence in me.

Make a non-restrictive buyer's representation agreement part of your marketing plan. Do a great job for your buyers. Have some confidence in your skills. If you lose an occasional buyer, so what? It happens. There will be plenty more, I assure you.

Give Them My Book for Buyers

Buyer agents across the country are using my bestselling book as a promotional/educational tool. My company, HelpUBuy America, has been in business for 20 years, and we have a rock solid reputation. Forming an alliance with us gives you credibility and gives your prospect a clear picture of how you will be working with them to accomplish their goal. I give a copy to any buyer who takes the time to meet with me. You can order discounted copies through me at Alysse@HelpUBuyAmerica.com. You can get a preview on Amazon.com or at Barnes and Noble. The name of the book is Buying a Home: Don't Let Them Make a Monkey Out of You!

Sign State-Mandated Documents, if any

The Texas Real Estate Commission requires Texas Realtors to discuss our agency relationship and to sign the Information About Brokerage Services Documents at our first meeting, Understand and fulfill the legal requirements in your state.

Collect a Deposit

You may wish to collect a small deposit ($100) from potential buyers to ensure that they are sincere in their efforts to purchase a home through you. This weeds out the time wasters.

If you want to see a fight break out, bring up the topic of deposits to a group of Realtors. The desperate, big box agents will claim it is "unheard of" to expect a buyer to pay a deposit; the agent asking for the deposit must be a crook! Not true, of course. I'm not a crook. But I'm not a person who likes my time wasted, either. Collecting a deposit goes a long way to ensure that doesn't happen. My policy on deposits is as follows:

- The deposit is 100% refundable at closing.
- If the buyer fails to buy a house through us for any reason, they lose their deposit.
- In the event that we choose to release them as clients, we will return the money to them in full. Things that might cause us to release a client are: showing up late on a regular basis, cancelling too many appointments, not providing a pre-approval letter, backing out of multiple contracts, or simply being difficult to work with.

Remember that you don't have to work with anyone you don't like. Pick and choose your clients; you're working as a volunteer until payday. In time, you'll learn how to weed out the time wasters or PITAs (Pains in the A*%) early on in the process. How? Pay attention to how buyers treat you when they are initiating contact with you. If they are leaving you urgent messages every hour from 9pm until midnight because they saw a house on Zillow and they must see it immediately, working with them might not be a lot of fun. If they call you at 7am and insist on seeing a house at 9am, they might be a problem client in the future. If you have to make an appointment to get your haircut, you have to make an appointment with me. I'm not a beck and call girl.

Generally speaking, however, buyers will be excited to have found you and will consider themselves lucky to work with you. Remember that you are offering a unique service. Don't let crazy-making clients make a monkey out of you!

Communicate by Email

Email should be your preferred method of communication for several reasons. First, it gives you time to respond to buyer's requests. You won't always know the answer to your client's questions, and quite often you'll need to be behind your computer to get the information they need. Email gives you time to think or get help to find the correct answer. Second, most of our clients have no idea how to buy a home. They confuse the terminology and are not always able to correctly communicate the details of the transaction to other parties (lender, title, spouse). Third, accuracy is critical! We need to be absolutely sure that offers/counteroffers accurately convey our client's wishes. Mistakes made will come out of your pocket, not theirs! Confirm it all in writing. And lastly, if there is ever a dispute with a client about your handling of their file, you will have written documentation to backup your claims. I'm not a person who is overly concerned about covering my tracks, but reducing everything to writing goes a long way in defending yourself against claims and accusations made about you. I have copies of all my business communications forwarded to my Gmail account automatically, just in case. I've never had a complaint filed against me, but I have had clients ask me for various receipts or documents years after they have closed on their house. I'm always able to retrieve what they need via my Gmail account and that makes me a hero. I like being a hero.

House Hunting

A very common complaint about Realtors is this: "I signed their agreement and have been waiting for them to show me homes. I've had to select all the homes and ask her to show them to me." Or, they complain when their Realtor sends them home listings and expects them to go through the list.

The problem here is communication. It's vital that you and your buyer come to agreement on how you will work together. Are they flat-fee buyers expecting full-service treatment? Are their expectations reasonable? Discuss these issues upfront and at your very first meeting. Be clear of their expectations are so that you can provide the level of service that they desire and require. The ways that I choose to work with buyers are discussed next.

Pick a House, Any House

I like to have my buyers choose the homes that interest them, at least initially. It helps me learn their likes and dislikes, allowing me the opportunity to learn what might appeal to them.

Home Finder Auto Search

The Home Finder service (described earlier) is set up for your buyer on the MLS. Once the buyer's requirements are entered in the computer, the buyer will receive new listings and status changes automatically, once a day. Home Finder allows the client to sort the listings according to Favorites, Possibilities, and Rejects, and allows them to ask you questions and make comments about any home in their 'portal.' They can view photos, take virtual tours, and see the home on a map to rule out homes in bad locations. Home Finder makes working with your buyer easy, and the clients love it. Chances are, the same type of service is available (for free) through your local board. If not, your first order of business every day is to send your clients any new listings that might suit their needs.

Buyer Requests a Showing

After the buyer selects the homes that interest them, they should contact you to request a tour. In a seller's market, last minute shows are a necessity. Generally speaking, however, it's smart to require them to request showings at least 48 hours in advance. Remember to keep track of the homes that you show them and the number of trips that you make to do so.

Preliminary Research on Homes

We have access to information that the buyer doesn't. Disclosures, surveys, engineer reports, and other information are sometimes available on the MLS for Realtor eyes only. Take care not to 'waste' their 12 showings. Check the location on Google maps. Look at the disclosure and see if there are any major problems with the property. Don't show the house if there is evidence of an issue that would make the house a "dog," like foundation repairs, backs up to power lines, a busy street, commercial property, railroad tracks, etc. Tell them you've uncovered an issue and share the reports with them; advise them to pass. If they still want to see it, show it, but send them an email warning them of the potential issues. But ultimately, it's their decision.

Schedule the Showing

Generally, schedule showings within a 1- to 2-hour window, unless the seller has special requirements. Explain that most houses are occupied and the sellers are vacating the property for their benefit. It's rare that a buyer will 'no show,' but common that they arrive a little late, so plan accordingly. Assuming you have already screened your buyer, plan your route and meet them at the first house. They can either follow you or ride with you from there. If you are only viewing a few homes, it's usually easier to have them follow you.

Centralized Showing Service is a scheduling service used by most agents in Texas and across the country. Chances are a service like this is available in your area. Listing agents love it because they don't have to schedule the appointments with their sellers, and buyer agents love it because all showings can be scheduled online or with a single phone call. The service is free for buyer agents, but not listing agents.

What to Bring to Showings

Because the buyer has carefully handpicked the houses that interest him/her (flat-fee clients), it is reasonable to provide as much information as possible about each home you show. Try to bring the following when you meet, but only if the information is readily available on the MLS:

- MLS Listing - Bring two copies of the Agent Full Report (one for you, one for the buyer). This report includes information that is generally only available to Realtors. We always share this information with our buyers.

- Sellers Disclosures
- Engineers Reports, if any
- Survey, if readily available

When working with full-service clients, it's generally enough to bring two copies of the MLS listing and the seller's disclosure, if it is readily available. If they like a particular home, you can provide them more information later.

Showing Homes Like an EBA

Unless you're working with a full-service buyer where you preview homes before you show them to your client, you will be visiting the home for the first time with them. If you've ever worked with a traditional Realtor, you know that their focus is to highlight the positives in the house and hide the faults. Our job is the opposite; we point out the negatives first and the positives second. Warn your buyers in advance that we work this way because it can be a little unsettling to some buyers. I've been dubbed a 'buzz kill' on more than one occasion.

The following sections describe what you should discuss with every buyer on your first tour.

Flooring

Buyers have strong preferences when it comes to flooring. It's important to know the various types and approximate cost of each.

Carpet

There are many different types of carpet including cut pile, Saxony, velvet, frieze, Berber, and more. It's not really necessary to know all the different types, and it's pretty easy to spot a carpet that it is in good condition vs. carpet that is stained and worn. Carpet is almost always found in the bedrooms and sometimes in the bathrooms. Some buyers will take issue with carpet in the bathrooms for obvious reasons. If the carpet is worn, it's better to get a carpet allowance rather than requesting that the seller replace it. In an effort to save money, sellers will put in the poorest quality carpet and pad. The house will look great at closing, but like garbage in 6 months.

Vinyl Flooring

Vinyl flooring is an inexpensive alternative to ceramic tile and is commonly used in wet areas like the kitchen, laundry room, and bathrooms. It is available in a huge variety of colors and styles. Expect to see vinyl flooring in kitchens of lower-priced homes, and sometimes in bathrooms and laundry rooms of moderate-priced homes. Generally speaking, vinyl is considered a lower-end, budget product, although a good quality vinyl floor can be rather pricey.

Laminate Flooring

Laminate flooring (brand name Pergo) looks like wood, but it is actually a synthetic product. These types of floors are floating floors, meaning the planks are not glued to the slab like real wood. As a result, when you walk on a laminate floor, it sounds hollow. Laminate flooring is easier to care for than real wood, and it is far more durable and less expensive. Laminate flooring gets mixed reviews. It is very important to know the difference between a real wood floor and a laminate flooring product since you don't want your client to assume the flooring is wood when it is not.

Hardwood Flooring

Solid hardwood floors are made of planks milled from a single piece of timber. These floors have a thicker wear surface and can be sanded and finished more times than an engineered wood floor. Wood floors in wet areas are generally considered to be a bad idea since water can cause the wood to warp.

Engineered Wood Flooring

Engineered wood floors have real wood on the top layer and composite wood on the bottom. It can be difficult to tell the difference between a solid wood floor and an engineered wood floor. An engineered wood floor is far less expensive than a solid wood floor.

Ceilings

You will encounter different types of ceilings when looking at homes. The following are some of the types you will see.

Acoustic Ceilings

Acoustic ceilings are also known as popcorn ceilings or cottage cheese ceilings. All these terms refer to the spray on ceiling treatment commonly used in older homes. It was originally used to hide imperfections in the ceiling and for its noise reduction qualities. Some lower-end builders still use this treatment today because it is far less expensive to finish a ceiling this way than it is to create a smooth surface. Although popcorn ceilings are not a deal killer for most buyers, some will refuse to purchase a house with this type of treatment, or they will hire a service to remove and refinish the surface of the ceiling.

Cathedral Ceilings

A cathedral ceiling is a ceiling that has a center point higher than the walls. This is the most common type of upgrade to the ceiling structure and goes a long way to increasing the overall perception of room size.

Vaulted Ceilings

A vaulted ceiling has one wall of the room taller than the opposing wall. The ceiling slants down to the lowest wall, again giving the impression or illusion that the room is larger than it is really is due to the increased volume.

Countertops

Today's homeowners have more countertop options then ever before. The next section describes these options.

Granite

Granite is very popular. Generally speaking, it stands up to heavy use and is resistant to heat and cutting. It can chip or crack, and most granite has to be sealed to prevent staining. Prices can range from $35 to $200 per square foot.

Limestone

Limestone is resistant to heat, but cracks and stains easily because it is highly porous. It is beautiful, but pricey at $60 to $100 per square foot.

Marble

Although beautiful, marble is one of the least durable stones you can use inside a home. It's liable to stress fractures and is easily scratched. It also will begin to deteriorate when exposed to acidic substances like lemon juice or vinegar. Marble is very expensive and is best strictly for decorative accents like a backsplash, or used in low traffic areas like guest bathrooms or the entryway. Onyx is a type of marble that is translucent; it is also best used strictly for decorative purposes.

Quartz (Engineered Stone)

Quartz is one of the hardest minerals in nature. Countertops made from it are very strong and durable. Quartz countertops aren't solid stone, though. They're a manufactured composite made up of quartz embedded in a hard-drying epoxy. The resulting material looks like stone and wears better than any other countertop material on the market. Engineered stone products get top marks for scratch resistance, heat resistance, and easy maintenance. You can find engineered quartz like the Silestone quartz countertops priced between $50 and $100 per square foot.

Concrete

Currently touted as an eco-friendly choice for kitchen design, concrete countertops are gaining in popularity. They offer lots of options for dyeing and texturing. They have to be sealed periodically to keep them from staining, though, and they are susceptible to chipping and cracking. Coming in at $80 to $120 per square foot, concrete is a high-end choice.

Tile

Tile is heat and stain resistant, but it's prone to chipping and cracking. Discolored and deteriorating grout can cause difficulties, too. Buyers can avoid some of these problems by sticking with quality ceramic and porcelain tile manufactured for heavy duty use and opting for a narrow grout tile design, or a layout that uses dark instead of light grout. It is common these days to see granite tiles that give the look of granite slab at a much lower price.

Solid Surface Synthetics

Acrylic countertops blend functionality with an attractive appearance. They can look like stone or be a solid color, but for a price that's just a bit higher than a high-end laminate. If a solid synthetic surface is scratched, it can easily be repolished. Unlike a laminate that has a thin surface "finished" layer, solid surface countertops have a continuous thickness that can be buffed and resurfaced as needed. Brand names are Samsung, Staron, and Corian. Buyers can expect to pay $35 to $100 per square foot.

Laminate (Formica)

Easy to install and available in lots of colors and patterns, laminate is a versatile and budget-friendly countertop choice. It has other advantages, too. You can find seamless designs that look quite beautiful. And, laminate countertops are heat and scratch resistant and are highly durable. The cost is between $10 and $30 per square foot.

Appliances

Built-in appliances are included in the sale of the home. Anything that can be unplugged and carried away (refrigerator, washer/dryer, countertop microwaves) will be removed from the property when the seller moves. The following sections describe all you really need to know about appliances.

Stainless Steel vs. White/Black/Almond

Stainless steel appliances are the current trend, but homeowners are learning that keeping them free of fingerprints and smudges is a daily chore. White appliances tend to yellow over time, and almond is considered a bit dated. Generally speaking, the colors of all the appliances should be the same...all stainless, all black, etc., but they can be different brands.

Gas vs. Electric

The benefit to cooking with an electric oven is that heat is distributed evenly. Electric ovens also heat very accurately; if you set it to 350 degrees, it stays at 350 degrees. Gas is cheaper to cook with than electric, but the savings aren't massive. Still, lots of chefs love cooking with gas because the heat is easier to control with gas, the kitchen doesn't get as hot, and on an electric stove, the pot has to be perfectly flat for the heat to be distributed evenly. Gas is more forgiving in this area.

Single Ovens

Single ovens will fit pretty much anywhere in your kitchen – whether it's under a counter or in an eye level cabinet. There may only be one oven to bake, roast, and grill in, but there's usually enough space to cook most things. Single ovens can be built-in or have a range top.

Double Ovens

There are two types of double ovens: a double built-in and the smaller double built under. The only real difference is in how tall they are. Double ovens can have a range top, but are more often built into the wall.

Compact Ovens

Compact ovens are a good option if space is at a premium in the kitchen – they're smaller than single ovens and are roughly the same size as a large built-in microwave. They usually come with an oven and grill and are often found in higher-end homes used as warming drawers.

Range top vs. Cooktop

A range top has a more professional chef look than a cooktop. Cooktops have a streamlined look. Both require a separate oven. Adequate ventilation is imperative, and a kitchen vent out is highly recommended (see next section).

Range Hoods/Ventilation

There are different types of vents that remove smoke, heat, and odors away from the kitchen when you cook. A recirculating vent uses a filter to clean the air before releasing it back in to the house. An external vent takes the contaminated air outside through a vent or duct. The type of vent used is a very big issue to many buyers. People who cook with certain spices insist on an external vent. If a house doesn't have an external vent, one can sometimes be added depending on the location of the stove. If it is against an external wall, it is usually a pretty easy installation.

Cabinets

This section describes the types of cabinets you will see in various homes.

Basic Cabinets

Often called stock, these are inexpensive, off-the-shelf cabinets, ready to assemble and install. Many use frameless construction where the door has no lip or "reveal" around it. These are a money-saving choice if your buyers aren't too picky about style options or don't demand a perfect fit. More have better drawers, solid wood doors, and other once-pricey features, but many basic boxes are thinly veneered particleboard, rather than higher-quality plywood. Style and trim options, sizes, and accessories are still limited.

Mid-level Cabinets

These models are a sound choice for most kitchens. Many use face frame construction, where the solid wood frame shows around the door and drawers.

Mid-level models offer many made to order custom options including size, materials, finish, elaborate crown moldings and other trim, and accessories such as range hood covers. That can make them the best value option overall. As with basic cabinets, features and quality can vary considerably. Boxes may be veneered particleboard rather than higher quality plywood.

Premium/Semi-Custom Cabinets

Short of custom made-to-order cabinets, these mid-level, semi-custom models offer the most style and storage options. They generally come with plywood boxes and other premium materials and hardware. Widths may come in ¼-inch increments, rather than the typical 3 inches.

While generally less expensive than fully made-to-order custom units, models with the most features and highest quality can cost as much as some full-custom units.

Floor Plans

The flow of the house needs to make sense. You need the right number of rooms and a place for everyone in the family to work, play, and sleep. Because people live differently, floor plans are not "one size fits all." Here are some general rules that apply to most people:

Formal Living and Dining – Combo

I usually try to steer buyers away from the combo, or stacked plan (see Figure 1). In a combo plan, the formal living room and formal dining room are one large space, which takes up much of the front of the house. Most people do not want formal living space anymore, favoring home office space instead. In a combo plan, there is a lot of wasted space. Look for split formals (see Figure 2), rather than stacked formals. A split formal floor plan has the dining room on one side of the front door and the formal living room on the other. Adding French doors to the formal living room will transform it into a home office.

Figure 1: Living Room/Dining Room - Combo

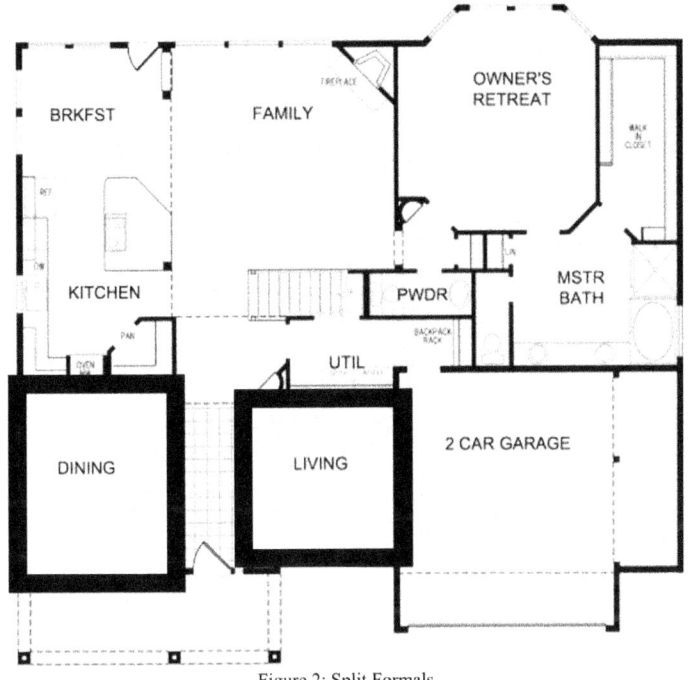

Figure 2: Split Formals

Open Concept Kitchen/Family Room

An open concept kitchen (Figure 3) is one in which the kitchen, breakfast room, and family room exist as one large space rather than smaller sectioned areas. Generally speaking, this type of space is very, very popular because the person cooking or cleaning the kitchen can watch the kids and isn't isolated from the happenings in the family room. The downside is that the cooking odors travel to the living space and that there is nowhere to hide the mess.

Figure 3: Open Concept Kitchen

Master Bedroom

A large percentage of newer homes have the master bedroom on the first floor. The perceived benefit is that the adults are downstairs and the kids are upstairs, so the downstairs area stays neater and quieter. Some buyers have learned the hard way that it is extremely inconvenient to have a new baby in a nursery on the second floor, away from Mom and Dad. The choice is theirs, of course. Today's buyers still favor a downstairs master, even knowing that the crib and changing table may end up in a corner in the master bedroom, at least for a while.

Be mindful of the location of the downstairs master bedroom. The location preferred by most is in the back of the house, but there should be at least a small hallway to separate the master bedroom from the family room (see Figure 4). In other words, you should not be able to look into the master bedroom from the family room.

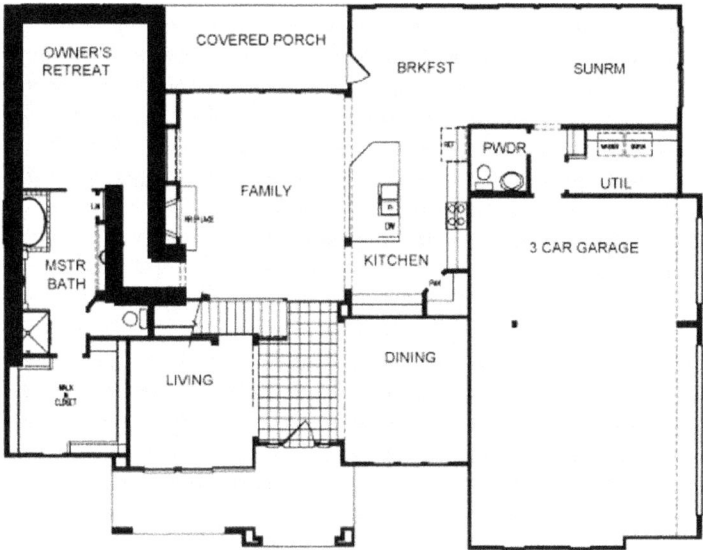

Figure 4: Master down with separation from family room

Master bedrooms located in the front of the house (see Figure 5) are not nearly as desirable as ones located in the back. Though not necessarily a deal killer, a significant number of buyers will walk away from this type of floor plan. An ideal and highly sought after floor plan is one with both the master and a second bedroom downstairs, and two or three bedrooms upstairs, as pictured next.

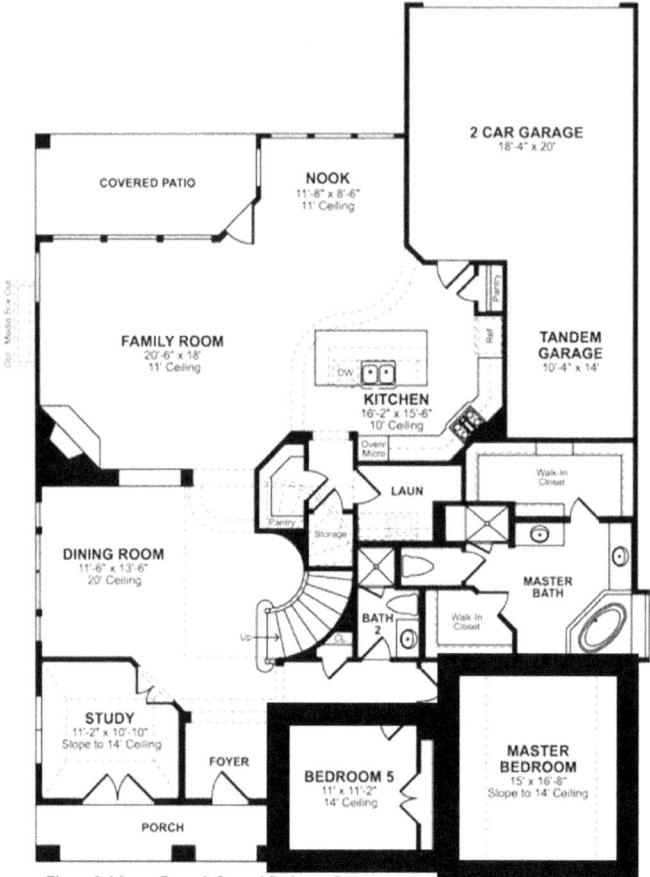

Figure 5: Master Front & Second Bedroom Down

Kitchen

An ideal floor plan is one in which the garage opens into the utility room, which leads to the kitchen, so you do not have to carry your groceries from the garage across the house to the kitchen (see Figure 6). Also illustrated in this example is the odd location of the utility room, next to the formal living spaces.

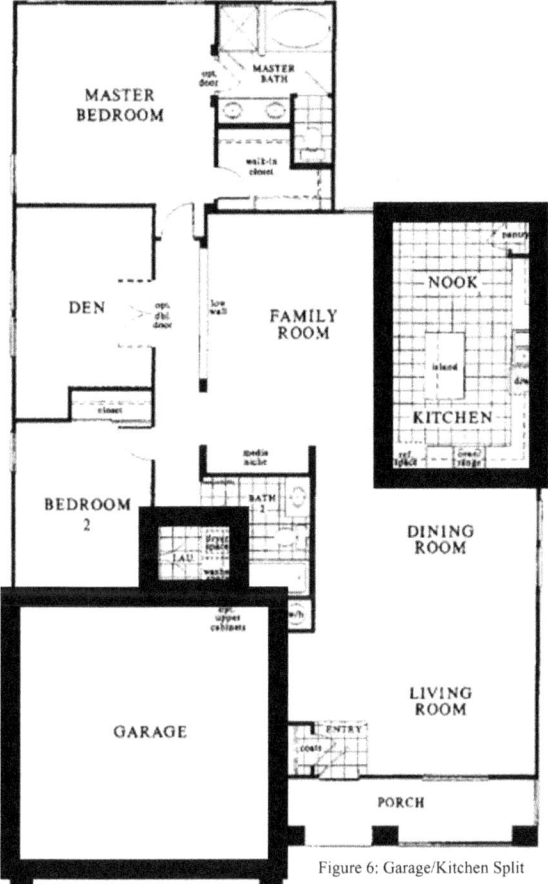

Figure 6: Garage/Kitchen Split

Split Bedrooms

In single-story homes, homes with a three-way split allow family members some privacy. As can be see in Figure 7, bedrooms are located on opposite sides of the home, separated by the family room.

Figure 7: Split Bedrooms

Construction Items

You do not need to be an inspector, but your clients must be able to rely on you to recognize basic defects in a home. The following sections describe some of the things you should know.

Roof

The following section describes the various types of roofing, and how to assess the condition of the roof from the ground.

Asphalt Shingles

Asphalt shingles are inexpensive to make, relatively easy to install, and widely available in all parts of the country. They are today's most popular roofing material—not only because they're less costly than wood, wood shakes, tile, metal or slate, but also because their guaranteed life span is roughly 20 to 30 years, depending on the quality of shingle purchased.

It's not your job to climb on top of the roof. But a lot can be learned about the roof from the ground. Look for the following:

- Areas where the roof sags
- Torn, curled, or missing shingles
- Shingle granules (they look like large grains of sand) in the gutters or around on the ground
- Examine the drainage, and make sure gutters and downspouts are securely attached
- Overlays. In the 1990s, it was common for roofers to attach a second layer of shingles rather than remove the old shingles and decking (insurance companies stopped paying for the removal of the old materials). Many insurance companies will refuse to provide coverage for homes with overlay roofs, which is ironic since they were the source of the original problem.

Wood Shingles

Wood shingles or shakes make a great roofing material that not only looks good, but resists insects, lasts for 25 or more years, sheds water, and provides better insulating value than composite shingles. While wooden shingles can be made from a variety of woods including redwood and pine, cedar is by far the most popular material for either shingles or shakes. Because of the increased fire hazard associated with wood roofs, the cost of homeowner's insurance tends to be higher.

Slate

Slate roofing tile is generally known as one of the highest-quality, longest lasting roofing materials on the market. On the other hand, it is very expensive, difficult to install, and the slate tends to be very fragile. In addition, slate is heavy. The housing structure must be able to support the extra weight.

Metal

Metal is the lightest material that can be installed on the roof. It offers great weather resistance and can last for 50+ years with little maintenance. The biggest downside to a metal roof is the cost.

Foundations

A foundation does more than just hold a house above ground. It also keeps out moisture, insulates against the cold, and resists movement of the earth around it. The next sections discuss the two types of foundations and how to determine if they are in need of repair.

Concrete Slab

Foundations crack. That's why the foundation is usually composed of steel in concrete — to hold it together when it does. The key is knowing why the crack as there and whether or not it might be an indication of a larger problem. Your job is not to guarantee the condition of the foundation, but you must be able to recognize obvious foundation issues and know when to advise your buyer to walk away from the property.

The key to taking care of a home's foundation is to ensure that the moisture level is the same all the way around the house. The soils present throughout Texas have a tremendous capacity to absorb (and lose) water. This means that the soil will swell when it is very wet, and it will shrink when it is very dry. This creates significant stresses on the concrete slab, which is resting on top of the soil. Keeping the soil around the home's foundation at a constant moisture level with soaker water hoses will help reduce the chances of needing house leveling in the future.

There are other causes, such as poor compaction of the soil by the original builder. Poor soil compaction will usually create foundation problems during the first 1 to 5 years of the home's life. Under slab plumbing leaks can be another source of foundation problems. Usually, older homes are more likely to have under slab plumbing leaks because their cast iron or concrete pipes have reached the end of their useful lives. If there is a settlement of soil under the interior or exterior portions of a home's foundation, then it may create a void between the soil and the bottom of the slab foundation. When this void becomes too large, the slab foundation can collapse (settlement) because there is nothing supporting it. Note: Slab cracks in the corners of the house are common and generally nothing to worry about.

Pier and Beam Foundation

A pier and beam foundation offers greater stability in areas where there is a lot of soil movement, and they are far less expensive to repair than a concrete slab should a repair be required. It is imperative that these foundations be vented property to avoid excess moisture, which may lead to wood rot. The floors can creak and move and feel unstable if there is too much flexibility in the wood. The cost to build a home with a pier and beam foundation is substantially higher than it is to build a home with a concrete slab.

Windows

There are many different styles of windows that are available in a number of different materials.

Wood Windows

Windows were traditionally made of wood, and wood is still popular because of its versatility. If old windows are drafty, you can install weather stripping. Hardwood is expensive, but is durable and only needs the protection of oil. You can also paint hardwood windows or give them a natural finish. Softwood windows need to be protected by paint or a natural wood finish, and regularly maintained.

Vinyl Windows

Double-glazed, vinyl windows offer excellent heat and sound insulation. Old windows are often replaced throughout the house with new vinyl windows. In addition to white and almond, other finishes are available, such as wood grain. Vinyl requires very little maintenance, and replacing old aluminum windows (discussed below) can save a homeowner a substantial amount of money on their heating and cooling expenses.

Aluminum Windows

Where maximum light is required, aluminum windows can be an excellent option since the strength of aluminum means a thin frame can support a large expanse of glass. However, aluminum conducts heat out of the home and is prone to condensation. Double glazing may be required by building regulations to reduce heat loss.

Double Pane vs. Single Pane

Double-pane windows have two layers of glass with inert gas in between the panes. Single pane has only piece of glass. Double-pane windows are by far more energy efficient than single pane. However, when the seals around the two pieces of glass pop, gas can get in between the two panes of glass and cause condensation. There is no way to fix the window; the glass needs to be replaced.

Air Conditioning

It is wise to understand how air conditioners work. Here are the basics:

The typical central air conditioning system is a split system, with an outdoor air conditioning, or "compressor bearing unit," and an indoor coil, which is usually installed on top of the furnace in the home. Using electricity as its power source, the compressor pumps refrigerant through the system to gather heat and moisture from indoors and remove it from the home. Heat and moisture are removed from the home when warm air from inside the home is blown over the cooled indoor coil. The heat in the air transfers to the coil, thereby "cooling" the air. The heat that has transferred to the coil is then "pumped" to the exterior of the home, while the cooled air is pumped back inside, helping to maintain a comfortable indoor temperature. Central air conditioning can also be provided through a package unit or a heat pump.

Most indoor units are located either in the attic or a hall closet. If the unit is easily accessible, you can read the label to confirm the age of the system. The outdoor unit is located outside, hopefully in a location that doesn't interfere with the enjoyment of the backyard. You can look for rust and read the label of the outside unit to assess its general condition. If you note that the air conditioning units are old and possibly rusted, advise your buyer to pay a little less for the house. But leave it to the inspector to diagnose any a/c related issues.

Exterior Materials

Exterior materials help to create an attractive outer finish for a home and serve as its first line of defense against wind and rain. The materials underneath it ensure that the home stays safe and structurally sound. The various types of exterior materials are discussed below.

Stucco and EIFS (synthetic stucco)

Real stucco is a highly durable product that can last a lifetime. It's basically cement and lime that is applied over chicken wire on the exterior of the house. Stucco, unlike wood siding, never needs to be painted. It is maintenance free and worry free for years to come. Stucco adds an excellent R-value (insulation efficiency), helping to keep the home cooler in the summer months and to keep out the harsh winds of winter, in turn, saving on both heating and cooling costs.

Synthetic stucco or EIFS (Exterior Insulation Finishing System) is a nightmare that should always be disclosed to buyers. EIFS has been associated with high moisture readings in the structural wood components of properties clad with this product. High moisture levels often lead to problems such as rot damage and termite infestation. The problem is aggravated by the fact that the damage occurs behind the EIFS siding and can be difficult to detect. To tell the difference between real stucco and synthetic stucco, knock on it. EIFS is relatively light and sounds hollow when tapped. Real stucco is heavy and feels and sounds solid when tapped. Some insurance companies won't insure homes where EIFS is used. If you are helping someone buy a home where EIFS is involved, take the following steps to protect your buyer:

- Confirm that the house is insurable by calling a few insurance agents
- Check with your buyer's lender to confirm that the loan won't be denied.
- Hire a licensed EIFS inspector to ascertain the condition of the exterior walls. A normal inspector is not qualified to inspect EIFS.

Brick

Brick homes can be solid brick or brick veneer. Homes older than roughly 40 years are more likely to be solid brick, while newer homes are almost certainly brick veneers. Solid-brick houses (also known as double-brick and solid-masonry houses) are built from either two layers of brick, or a layer of concrete block and an adjacent layer of brick on the exterior. A brick-veneer home is built with wood or steel framing. A single layer of brick is built near the frame and then attached to the house with metal ties. If you removed bricks from a solid-brick house, the house would fall down. Conversely, if bricks were removed from a brick-veneer home, the house would remain standing.

Brick is a naturally energy-efficient material and can withstand substantial winds. It is extremely low maintenance and lasts far longer than other materials.

Siding

Siding is made of horizontal or vertical boards that are attached either directly to the building structure (studs) or to an intermediate layer of wood. The types of siding are discussed below.

Vinyl Siding

Vinyl siding is the most commonly used siding in new, single-family homes. It is the least expensive siding option and comes in a variety of colors and levels of quality, although it cannot be painted. It is known to be flammable and releases toxins if burned. That's generally not a selling point.

Cement Siding

Cement siding is a mix of sand and cement. It is much thicker than vinyl and can withstand harsh weather like wind or hail far better than vinyl. It is resistant to termites, holds paint well, and is mostly maintenance free. Cement siding (brand name Hardiplank) is commonly used in new homes. It's an excellent product and commonly seen in new construction.

Wood Siding

Wood siding requires painting every five to ten years and can warp when exposed to excessive moisture. It is a green option, made primarily from recycled wood and smaller, quick-growing trees. Because of the maintenance involved with wood siding, it is considered to be the least desirable siding option.

Property Condition – Be on the Lookout

To have a successful career as an Exclusive Buyer Agent, it is imperative that you are able to spot obvious flaws in the condition of the home and are able to recognize unpopular floor plans. That's your job, and your clients rely on you to do it well.

My personal guarantee to my buyer/clients is that if the inspection uncovers something that leads them to walk away from the house, I will pay for their next inspection. I suggest you adopt the same policy.

The following includes some general guidelines on what to look for when evaluating a property. Note that different materials are used in different parts of the country, and this list is not meant to be all-inclusive.

Roof

If the asphalt roof is more than 15 to 20 years old, chances are it needs to be replaced. But younger roofs can also fail. Look for shingles that are lifting up, cracked, have curled edges, or are even missing altogether, and take note of areas where the granules have worn off. Also look for water stains on the underside of the roof and on the ceiling. Although it's not your job to walk the roof, it's important to know its general condition before writing an offer.

Foundation

Foundation problems are usually caused by bad drainage, ground movement, or poor construction, which causes the foundation to shift or settle. Signs of foundation problems include doors and windows that no longer open or close, drywall cracks, and cracks in the bricks. Less obvious clues are cracks in the slab that can sometimes be seen on vinyl floors, cracked tiles that do not lay flat, and a slanted floor.

Sprinkler

It is very common for sprinkler heads to break, usually when someone runs over them with the lawn mower. The control box located in the garage turns the system on and off, and is usually zoned for front, back, and the sides of the house. Be certain you know how much of the yard is sprinklered. Some homes only have sprinklers installed in one area of the yard. You do not want your buyer to overpay for the home because you have mistakenly assumed the yard is fully sprinklered.

Air Conditioners and Heaters

Your inspector will test the heater and air conditioner to verify their operability, but it is important that you get an idea of their age and general condition before you make an offer. If your buyer will have to replace the air conditioner in the next few years, they shouldn't pay top dollar for the house. Take a look at both the inside and outside units, and take note of dust and rust in the vents. Improper maintenance will significantly shorten the life of heating and cooling systems. If the units are very old or seem to be neglected (dust in the vents), be sure to factor the replacement cost into your offer.

Windows

When air gets between the two pieces of glass in a double-pane window, the condensation can cause foggy windows. The only fix for this is to replace the glass. Your inspector will check each and every window, but try to get a general idea of their condition before you make an offer. If the house needs all new windows, the cost will run into the thousands.

Termites/Carpenter Ants

Termites and carpenter ants are similar in that they both destroy wood. Termites eat wood, and carpenter ants find dead, damp wood to build nests. There are two types of termites commonly found in the US; subterranean termites that live underground and dry wood termites that live in dry wood and can be found in framing, furniture, hardwood floors, and elsewhere.

Contrary to popular belief, termites are active throughout the year and not just in the spring. The most visible sign of termite activity is swarming, but there are other signs:

- Hollow-sounding wood
- Groups of winged insects
- Cracked paint on wood surfaces where they enter
- Mud tubes on exterior walls

You're not an inspector, and it's not your job to search the entire house for signs of termites or termite damage, but you should be able to recognize termites when you see them.

The lender may require a certificate from the inspector stating that the home is free of termites and other critters. Even if it is not a lender requirement, you will definitely want to know if the home has an active termite infestation or has been treated in the past. If prior treatments to the property have occurred, find out if they were partial treatments or if the whole house was treated. Sometimes if only one side of the house is treated, the termites will simply move from one side of the house to the other.

Plumbing

The inspector will check the plumbing system, but take note of leaking faucets, showerheads, and toilets, and also ascertain the age of the water heater by looking at the label on the unit. If the water heater is old and located in the attic, you will want it replaced by the seller, since a leak will damage the inside of the house. If it is located in the garage, gas water heaters must be on a stand eighteen inches off the floor, and they must have an expansion tank. Straps are required in earthquake zones.

Exposure

The direction a house faces is called its "exposure," and is a matter of personal preference. In some cultures, an east-facing home is considered lucky and the buyer will not consider any other exposure. If the front of the house faces north, the back yard has more sun in the summer. Homes facing south generally have shade in the backyard in the afternoon, which is desirable in warmer climates. The floor plan and location of the rooms will determine the comfort level of the home.

Lead-Based Paint

Homes built before 1978 may have been painted with lead-based paint. The seller or their agent is required to give the buyer the EPA booklet called "Protect Your Family From Lead in Your Home".

The seller must disclose any known lead-based paint hazards and turn over any relevant records. The risk with lead-based paint is when children or pets ingest it, since the lead can cause brain damage. Typically, homes that originally had lead-based paint have been repainted many times through the years and this reduces the risks substantially.

Environmental Hazards

Sellers are also required to disclose any known environmental hazards like leaking underground oil tanks, the presence of radon or asbestos, and lead pipes, among others. There can be serious health and financial consequences associated with the clean up of these hazards. It's your job to alert buyers of the environmental hazards in your area.

Floodplains

The buyer needs to know if the home is located in a floodplain. If it is, their lender is going to require flood insurance. The extra expense may or may not be a deal breaker, but they are entitled to know their risks and responsibilities before they sign on the dotted line. Go to http://www.floodsmart.gov/floodsmart/ to review the flood maps in your area.

Nuisance Factors

When you are at the house, listen for things that can make homeowners crazy, like barking dogs, traffic from local schools or restaurants, airplanes, trains, and noise from distant freeways. Remember, even if it doesn't bother your buyers during the day, the noise may drive them crazy at night. It's their decision, but it's your job to recognize it and make them aware.

Narrowing Down the List

The truth is that the perfect house does not exist. Even people who build a custom home find things they wish they had designed differently. With any luck, your buyers will find themselves with a short list of two or three homes. So, how do you help them decide which home to buy?

As they did in the old days, get out your old yellow legal pad. First, draw a line down the middle of the page and write the positive aspects of a prospective house on one side and the negative aspects on the other side; each finalist gets their own page. Hopefully, you have already eliminated homes in bad locations, with bad foundations and unlivable floor plans, and you are left with homes that are perfectly safe investments with good potential for resale. Have your buyers rank their choices, and compare and contrast the top two, as discussed later.

A Word About Resale

The secret to buying a home with good resale potential is to buy one that will attract the largest pool of buyers. Stated differently, don't buy a home that has a feature that no one in his or her right mind would want! That means none of the following: homes in bad locations, such as next to busy streets, schools, commercial property, power lines; homes without a garage, pantry, or linen closet; homes that have the smallest yard in the neighborhood; and/or homes with small closets, etc. The owners of these types of homes will try to distract your buyers with beautiful landscaping, hardwood floors, and stainless steel appliances, and will more than likely be priced a little lower than other homes in decent locations. Don't let your client buy someone else's problem! If they insist on buying it anyway, send them something in writing (preferably email) expressing your concerns. Keep this letter; you might need to refer to it in the future when they can't sell their house and they blame it on you.

Research the Property

You still need more information about the buyer's top choices before you can make a firm recommendation. Run the following reports and share them with your buyer:

Tax Rolls

The county tax appraisal websites have lots of information that is relevant to buyers. Become very familiar with the information on your county's site and learn how to find the following information, which should be given to your buyer before a contract is written.

Square Footage

Before a homebuilder can begin construction on a new home, they must file their plans with the city and obtain a permit. The square footage of the home that they plan to build is included in these plans. Sometimes the builder makes adjustments to the floor plans that affect the final size of the home and therefore the price. Always check the square footage of the home on the MLS and find out the source of the information.

If the source says, "taxes," verify that the MLS listing matches the tax rolls. A difference of even 100 square feet can translate into a thousand dollars or more. Ultimately it is the buyer's appraiser that will verify the square footage of the home.

Prior Owners

It really doesn't matter how many people owned a particular house, but it is information that interests the buyers. You should be able to learn when the seller purchased the house and from whom, and how many other previous owners there were. You can often find out how much the seller paid and the amount of his or her original loan. It helps to know how much equity a homeowner has, if you can figure it out. If, for example, the seller owes more than what the house is worth at today's prices, the seller is "upside down" and will need to take money to the closing table. You need to make sure that they have the cash to sell the house. If not, you're dealing with a short sale transaction, which is a whole different animal.

Taxing Trends

A good amount can be learned by looking at how the taxing authorities valued the property in prior years. If the Tax Assessed Value (TAV) was reduced for several years in a row, the home is in a neighborhood that is depreciating. If the area is in decline, try to find out why. Were there a lot of foreclosures or another problem in the neighborhood? Look at prior solds carefully and see if anything can be learned. If the TAV is steady or rises slightly for a few years, no further investigation is necessary.

Property Taxes

The local tax authorities in your area determine the value of a home for taxing purposes. DO NOT confuse tax-assessed value with fair market value. Taxable value and fair market value are two completely different types of valuations.

Fair market value is based on the sale prices of other properties, not the taxable values of other properties. Buyers commonly assume that the taxable value is the price they should pay for a home. Buying based on tax value is a flawed purchase model; it doesn't work for a great number of reasons. First, appraisal districts are capped at the amounts they can raise a taxable value over a given period of time and appraisal districts assign taxable values once each year. Fair market value fluctuates week-to-week, month-to-month, and sometimes daily. Fair market value is based on what has sold in the recent past, and what's traded in the free marketplace.

Buyers will ask why sellers list houses for so much over the assessed value. The answer is because the assessed value is not what the property is worth in the free market. It's the amount on which the taxes are based. It doesn't mean that the seller hasn't overpriced their property, but it does mean that trying to base a purchase offer on the tax assessment is a fight that most buyers will lose over and over again.

Homestead Exemptions (not in all states)

An exemption removes part of the value of the property from taxation and lowers the owner's taxes. For example, if the home is valued at $50,000 and the owner qualifies for a $15,000 exemption, the home is taxed as if it was worth only $35,000. Other than exemptions for disabled veterans or survivors, these exemptions apply only for the owner's homestead. They do not apply to other property a person may own.

There are several types of exemptions, including:

- School Taxes for All Homeowners - Most will qualify for a $15,000 homestead exemption on the home's value for school taxes.

- County Taxes for All Homeowners - If the county collects a special tax for farm-to-market roads or flood control, the homeowner will receive a $3,000 exemption for this tax. If the homeowner qualifies for local option exemptions for age 65 or older homeowners or disabled homeowners (next section), they will receive only the local option exemptions.

- Optional Exemptions for All Homeowners - Any taxing unit, including a school district, city, county, or special district, may offer an exemption up to 20 percent of the home's value. The amount of an optional exemption can't be less than $5,000, no matter what the percentage is. For example, if the home is valued at $20,000 and the city offers a 20 percent exemption, the exemption is $5,000, even though 20 percent of $20,000 is just $4,000. Each taxing unit decides whether it will offer the exemption and at what percentage. This percentage exemption is added to any other home exemption for which the homeowner may qualify. The taxing unit must decide before May 1 of the tax year to offer this exemption.

- Age 65 or Older Homeowners - If buyers are age 65 or older, the residence homestead will qualify for more exemptions, including a $10,000 homestead exemption for the school taxes on the home's value, in addition to the $15,000 exemption for all homeowners.

The presence or absence of homestead exemptions will have an effect on closing costs, tax prorations, and the cash to close.

Area Demographics and Factoids

Most agents have access to this type of information and can present it to their buyers in a pretty little package. You do not have to guess who your buyer's neighbors are; the information is out there for free! Use this information like pieces of a puzzle to learn everything you can about the property and area before you submit an offer for your buyer.

School Information

The MLS listing almost always indicates which schools are zoned to a particular property. But zoning can change. Ultimately, it's up to your buyer to investigate the schools, but I generally help them by sending them links to the school district and phone numbers for them to contact the administration. When providing information to your buyer about important things like schools, be sure to give them the source of your information.

Seller's Disclosure of Property Condition

It might be called something different in your state, but sellers are required by law to disclose everything that they know about the property. In Texas, they do so on a form promulgated by the Texas Real Estate Commission called the Seller's Disclosure of Property Condition. From this report, you will learn the age and condition of all of the components in the house.

Review this report very carefully with your buyers, and remember that the accuracy of these reports is contingent upon the seller's knowledge of the property and his or her integrity. Yes, some sellers lie in order to present their home in the best possible light. Shocking, I know. That's why you must insist that your buyer hire an inspector.

Engineer's Report

If sellers have hired a structural engineer to ascertain the condition of the foundation, they are required by law to share that information with the buyer. Try to encourage your buyer to buy a home without any structural issues. Send them the engineer reports with a strong warning that they should find another house. It's rare that a house is special enough to justify the risk involved with buying a home in poor structural condition. Don't try to interpret the information for them; we are not trained engineers. And always advise them to hire their own engineer before proceeding.

Survey

If the seller has a survey, they can share it with the buyer (in most states), saving them about $350. If the listing agent has put a copy of the survey on the MLS, give it to the buyer for their review. The sellers will deliver a copy of the survey and an affidavit stating that there have been no material changes to the property, like the addition of a swimming pool. If the seller's survey is unacceptable for some reason, the title company will let you know and will order a new one.

Comparative Market Analysis (CMA)

A CMA report is used to determine the value of the property. Believe me, it's an art and a science.

I highly, highly, highly recommend that you take an appraisal class; they are offered quite frequently and very inexpensively at your local board. The information I'm providing here is very general in nature. There are a million variables when it comes to pricing (area, cost of land and improvements), and it would be irresponsible and inaccurate of me to encourage readers to prepare a very important CMA based on my limited information. This is an area where you need additional and specific training. Having said all of this, here are the guidelines.

Although CMAs generally include active, pending, withdrawn, and expired listings, when pricing a property, we really only care about homes that are already sold. A seller might have listed his home for $400,000, but that doesn't mean someone is willing to pay that amount. We only care about what people actually paid for the property; these are the transactions that the banks have already approved.

To produce a CMA, first go onto the MLS and find comparable homes, preferably within the same subdivision. If there are no recent sales in the subdivision, try to find something within a few miles away. The following sections describe the criteria for comparable homes.

Square Footage

Square footage should not exceed more than 200 to 300 square feet, plus or minus. For example, if a house is 2000 square feet, try to find comparable homes that are in the range of 1700 to 2300 square feet. Look for homes that have the same exact footage as the home you are trying to buy. More often than not, they are the same floor plan.

Year Built

The age of the home should be within a few years of other each other.

Similar Upgrades and Condition

A home with a pool is worth more than one without a pool. A remodeled home is worth more than a fixer-upper.

Location

Homes with busy streets in the back are worth less than homes in the center of the neighborhood. If the subject home is next to railroad tracks, price adjustments need to be made in the CMA.

Sold Date

The comparable home should have been sold within the last 6 months.

CMA Software

Most real estate boards offer CMA software online as part of your membership. Other packages are available that are a lot prettier and easier to use. What matters most is the quality of the information you provide.

Here are the steps in creating a CMA:

1.   Research the subject property in the MLS. The "subject" property is the house your buyer wants to purchase. Make note of the subdivision name, square footage, age, condition, and whether or not it has a pool or oversized/undersized lot

2.   Search the MLS for comparable homes, as described in the previous section. Include active, pending, and sold statuses, but remember that only the solds affect the suggested purchase price.

3.   Adjust the sold properties to account for differences in amenities, size, bedrooms, lot, location, etc. This information is area specific! Talk to an appraiser in your area for detailed information.

Once you make all the adjustments, the software will perform the calculations and recommend a price range. Homes that are in pristine condition are valued at the top of the price range, and homes that need work will be in the lower end of the range or below, depending on the condition.

Your goal should be to select homes that are as similar as possible to your subject property so that minimal adjustments are necessary.

Offers and Negotiations

Ultimately, it's up to your buyers to decide what they are willing to pay, but as an Exclusive Buyer Agent, it's your job to provide them sufficient information to make an informed decision. The following items are things you should do before submitting an offer.

Call the Listing Agent

The first step in negotiating a contract is to call the listing agent to confirm that the house is still available. If it is, ask a few questions to encourage the listing agent to discuss the property. You're on a fishing expedition. You want to try to get him or her to reveal how motivated the seller might be to sell the property, and you want to look for other ways to get your buyer a better price and/or terms. Things you can ask are:

- How quickly does the seller need to move?

- Would it help the seller if the buyer let them lease the property back for a few weeks?
- Is there any flexibility in the price?

Technically, listing agents are supposed to keep quiet about their seller's level of motivation, but you'd be surprised how many will answer any question you ask. If they refuse to answer anything, you know you'll be negotiating against a well-trained agent. But even the best agents will let things slip or send you subtle clues about their client. If the listing agent responds, "Please, for the love of God, bring me an offer! Any offer!" you know you can make a lower offer. Most of them are far more professional than this, of course. There really is no secret code, as the Freakonomics people suggest, but Realtors are human after all. You can learn a lot in a friendly, five-minute conversation.

After asking about the seller, tell the agent that your buyer is very interested in the property, and mention that they have already obtained financing and can close quickly. Don't give specifics. You just want to get the listing agent excited about the offer in case other contracts come in; he or she will wait for yours instead of immediately selling the house to someone else.

Negotiating Strategies

Negotiating strategies will differ based on a number of factors including the desirability of the property and whether it's a buyer's market, a seller's market, or a balanced market. Let's look closer at the types of markets.

Seller's Market

Seller's markets are created when there are more buyers than houses; demand is greater than supply. In a seller's market, the best homes can generate multiple offers the first day it hits the market. Here are some general guidelines for getting your offer accepted in a seller's market:

- Make sure your buyer is pre-approved, not just pre-qualified. This means the buyer has made a formal loan application with a lender, their credit has been checked, and they have supplied the lender with sufficient documentation to support the claims they made on the loan application. A pre-qualification simply means the buyer calls a lender, tells them what their credit score is and how much they make, and then the lender tells them how much home they can afford to buy.
- Price is not always the most important factor, but generally speaking, your buyer will have to offer close to list price and sometimes even above. Remember that the house still has to appraise for at least the sales price or your buyer will have to make up the difference in cash. It's important to use an appraisal contingency in these situations.
- The amount of earnest money should be higher than normal.
- A larger option fee and shorter option period are preferred.
- Let the seller lease back the property for an extended period of time.
- Write a great cover letter.

Because there is more competition in a seller's market, you may have to write several contracts before your contract is accepted.

Buyer's Market or Balanced Market

In a buyer's market, there are lots of homes on the market but few buyers; supply is greater than demand. In this type of market, you want to write a contract that not only protects the buyer, but also favors the buyer. Here are some guidelines:

- The initial offer can be lower since there are few, if any, competing buyers.
- Buyer can offer less option money and a shorter option period.
- Earnest money can be lower.
- Buyer doesn't have to be as accommodating with possession. Allowing the seller 48 hours to move out after closing is sufficient.
- Buyer can ask for more repairs.
- If buyers are short on cash, they can request a seller contribution towards closing costs.

A balanced market, of course, is where there are equal numbers of buyers and sellers. Look for clues about the desirability of the property. How long has it been on the market? If it has been sitting a while, you can start your offer lower. Are there other homes for sale in the area that might work for your client? If so, you can offer less. If, however, it's the best house on the block and has only been on the market for a few days, your buyer will probably have to offer more. Write your offer based on what you learn.

Discuss different negotiating strategies with your buyer and let them make the choice. If their needs are highly specific, they may have to be more aggressive in their pricing and terms. If they have a backup property in the wings, they can try to get a better deal, since they have an alternate plan. The decision has to be theirs. It's very important, at this point, to begin to have all your communications in writing, if they aren't already. There is nothing more important than presenting the offer as your buyer intended it to be!

What to Negotiate

Although price is the primary consideration when negotiating a deal, there are others terms that the buyer and seller must agree upon, including the following:

Closing costs

If the buyer has enough money for their down payment, but not enough for their closing costs, it is possible for the sellers to pay up to 3% of the buyer's closing costs for them. Basically, the sales price is increased by the amount of the buyer's closing costs, and there is a "seller contribution towards closing." It is important that the buyer understands two things:

1.   The house must appraise for at least the sales price, or they will have to bring extra cash to cover the difference. In a competitive market where the sales price can often go above the list price, seller contributions towards closing costs make the seller nervous. These buyers are not as qualified in a seller's eyes as other buyers who have more cash – and they are right. It is possible for the lender to cover the buyer's closing costs, and this is sometimes a better way to go. Refer to the section entitled "All About Mortgages" in the Appendix of this book for more information. It should be noted that the buyer ultimately does pay their own closing costs, either in the form of a higher mortgage or a higher interest rate. No free rides!

2.   The Seller only cares about how much they are going to net in the transaction. They take the sales price, subtract their selling expenses, and look at their bottom line. They don't care how the deal is structured; they only care about how much money they will walk away with at closing. Take a look at the table below:

Offer One		Offer Two	
Sales Price:	$205,000	Sales Price:	$200,000
Seller paid closing costs:	$ 5,000	Seller paid closing costs:	$ 0,000
Seller's net proceeds	$200,000	Seller's net proceeds	$200,000

These two offers are the same in the eyes of the seller. But to a buyer who is low on cash, a $5,000 seller contribution towards closing costs is of vital importance.

Closing Date & Possession

Buyers need to understand how complicated life can be for any given seller. If the owner currently occupies the home, they can't buy a new house before the old one sells, and if they sell too quickly, they will have nowhere to go. Allowing the seller to lease the property back after closing is the single most effective way to win the contract if there are competing offers, and can even mean that your buyer pays less for the house.

The opposite is true if the seller has already moved and the house is vacant. In this case, they want to close as quickly as possible to alleviate the expense of maintaining more than one residence.

Repairs

Repairs are negotiated after the inspection. After the contract is executed, the buyer has their option period to get the home inspected and negotiate repairs. If there is something obviously in need of repair, it should be factored into your initial offer. Read the seller's disclosure of property condition carefully. If the seller has disclosed that the sprinkler system is broken, for example, include this repair in your initial offer.

Decorating Allowances

If the home is in need of new carpet, or if the walls and ceiling need to be painting, it's common for buyers to request a decorating allowance. It's usually best to have the decorating allowance apply towards the buyer's closing costs. This will reduce the amount that the buyer has to bring to closing, allowing them to use their cash for updates.

Home Warranty

The seller almost always buys a home warranty for the buyer, but in most cases the buyer chooses the warranty provider and the level of coverage. Some of the most popular home warranty companies are American Home Shield, Home Warranty of America, Choice Home Warranty, First American Home Warranty, Landmark Home Warranty, and Allied Home Warranty. Explain to your buyers that no warranty will cover every repair; chances are at least one of their claims will be rejected. In general, it's still smart to have unless the property is brand new. New construction homes generally have both structural and "bumper-to-bumper" warranties in place.

Title Company/Insurance

The title company is a neutral third party that manages the transaction after the contract is executed. They also issue the title policy that guarantees the chain of title.

It is very, very important that your buyer purchase title insurance. In my area, it's customary for the seller to buy the owner's title policy and for the buyer to buy the lender's policy. Both, of course, are negotiable.

There was a time where the seller always chose the title company. Things have recently changed. Now, Section 9 of the Real Estate Settlement Procedures Act prohibits sellers from conditioning the home sale on the use of a specific title insurance company. Violators can be subject to a very steep fine! Here are the details, from the NAR website:

If sellers pay for both the owner's and the lender's title insurance policies, they can require the use of a preferred title company.

If sellers pay for the owner's policy, they may insist on choosing a preferred title provider, but buyers must be free to select their own title company on the lender's policy (even if the cost of that lender's policy is higher than the fees charged by the seller's title company for the same policy).

Section 9 doesn't prohibit sellers from requiring the use of a particular title agent as long as the sellers don't own the title company. Make sure the language in the purchase contract makes clear that buyers, if they're paying for the title policy, are free to select their own title insurance company.

Most of my buyers could care less which title company we use as long as there is no affiliation between the parties. It's an easy point to let the seller win, but you always need to take direction from your buyer on this. If it's important to them that they select the title company, they are definitely entitled to do so.

Contingencies

A contingency in your contract will allow your buyer to back out of the deal without penalty if anything goes wrong. Some Realtors will say that buyers use them because they are not sure that they want to buy the house. These Realtors work for the seller. As an EBA, you don't want your buyer to spend money to inspect and appraise a home if the seller is not legally obligated to sell you the home once they do. Writing a contract with contingencies allows buyers the time they need to do their due diligence. Here are some common contract contingencies:

Financing Contingency

A financing contingency says that the offer is contingent upon the buyer being able to secure financing for the property within a certain period of time. It specifies in detail the type of financing, the terms, and how long they have to obtain loan approval. Unless your buyer is paying with cash, you should always include a Financing Contingency in your offer. If their financing falls through, at least they will get their deposit (earnest money) back. Generally, twenty days is plenty of time for them to secure financing. The deal does not have to close in twenty days, but they should have their loan approved with "conditions." Conditional loan approval means that the bank will lend them money once certain conditions are met, like the appraisal, job verification, a certain bank statement, and so forth.

Appraisal Contingency

The appraisal contingency has become an important one in recent days. The appraisal contingency says that if the house does not appraise for at least the purchase price, the buyer can back out of the deal. It can also be written to say that if the house doesn't appraise for the purchase price, the seller has to drop the price; if he or she refuses to do so, the buyer can back out of the deal without penalty. Truth be told, if the house does not appraise, the bank will not lend the buyer the money they need to buy the house. They will either have to pay cash for the difference (don't do this!), the seller will have to drop the price, or they will have to walk away from the deal. In any case, if there is a concern that the house won't appraise for at least the sales price, include an appraisal contingency.

Inspection Contingency/Option Period

Some states call this an "Option Period," and others call it a "Due Diligence Contingency." This contingency allows the buyer a certain period of time (I recommend 7 to 10 days) to get the home inspected, along with anything else they need to do to be certain that they want to buy the property. The buyer can back out of the deal for any reason at all without penalty, and he or she can use this period of time to renegotiate repairs with the seller after the inspection. Some states require that the buyer pay an "option fee" to the seller. Option fees are discussed later in this chapter.

Contingency for Sale of Another Property

This contingency is for buyers who have to sell their current homes before they can buy a new one. Basically, it allows the buyer the right to back out of the deal if he or she cannot sell their current home. Contracts can also be written with a "kick out" clause, which allows the seller to "kick out" the original contract if they find a new buyer that can close right away.

Earnest Money & Option Fee

An option fee is money paid by the buyer to the seller for the option to terminate the real estate contract. An option gives the buyer time to have the house inspected and negotiate repairs, while at the same time restricting the seller from selling the house to someone else. Buyers can terminate the contract during the option period for any reason. I write my contracts so the buyer loses their option fee if they terminate the contract, but get the money back if they close the transaction. The amount of the option fee is generally between $50 and $250 in my area. Note that not all states use options when buying and selling property, although everything is negotiable.

Option fee funds should not be confused with earnest money. Earnest money is a security deposit that demonstrates the buyer's commitment to purchasing the property and is a show of good faith. The amount of earnest money is negotiable. Generally, you want to keep the amount of earnest money to a minimum, but high enough that the seller takes your offer seriously.

Earnest money is applied to the buyer's down payment and closing costs. If there is a failure to close through no fault of the buyer, the seller usually signs an agreement to release the funds back to the buyer, and vice versa, if the seller fails to close. Disputes do arise, however, and that is when the buyer really needs to be able to rely on you to get their money back.

It's better to go low than high on the earnest money for a couple of reasons. First, the listing agent wants to look good in front of the seller and will almost always advise them to counter something, if for no other reason than to just show that they are doing their job. Earnest money is an easy thing for them to counter. Second, if for some reason the buyer loses his/her earnest money, we want this amount to be as low as possible. Best to start low and increase if the seller insists.

In a balanced market, lower-priced homes can get away with an option fee of $50 for a 10-day option period. Homes higher than $200,000 should offer $100 for a 10-day option. If the seller requires more money, they can ask for it in the form of a counteroffer.

Furniture and Appliances

It is common for the seller to offer to sell or leave some of their furniture and appliances for the buyer. It's important to be clear about the items that remain with the property and at what cost. If the seller agrees to leave the refrigerator, for example, write, "Refrigerator conveys at no additional cost to the buyer" in the special provisions section of the contract. Lenders don't like to see items like furniture and appliances rolled into the loan, so handle these in cash in a separate bill of sale.

Opening Offer

Give the CMA to your buyer, and have them come up with an opening offer. If the offer is ridiculous, tell them so, but you have to submit it anyway. If you think they can go lower, encourage them to do so. But in the end, let it be their decision and remember that you work for them. Review all of the above terms and come up with a negotiating strategy. Smart buyers will try to get the best price and most favorable terms by being flexible and by keeping the seller's needs in mind. Dumb buyers will try to nickel and dime the seller and antagonize them. As a result, these angry sellers are the ones who leave the house in poor condition for your buyers. Try to create a win/win situation. A word of warning here: Buyers will accuse you of negotiating on behalf of the seller if you work too hard to accommodate their needs. Explain the domino effect that is in place during these transactions, and remind them that it's better to have a deal with terms that the seller can live with so that they are out of the house on time, and so that they don't destroy it on the way out.

Writing and Presenting Your Offer

Because real estate law varies from state to state, writing contracts is far beyond the scope of this book, but what follows is the general process.

Contracts are created using a program like Zipforms and are basically fill in the blank. You can print them off and have your buyer sign them in person, or you can use the built-in electronic signature feature (assuming electronic signatures are legal in your state). Obtaining your client's signatures electronically makes it very easy to email your offer to the listing agent. Hardly anyone uses the fax machine anymore, and it's inconvenient for listing agents – who often work from home – to run up to their office to pick up a hard copy contract. Email makes it easy for everyone involved. Become proficient in writing contracts and in using the software; your local board more than likely offers classes in both. Be the agent who is easy to work with and whose buyers almost always close.

Pre-Approval Letter

You should have already received your buyer's pre-qualification or pre-approval letter before you showed them the first house. If more than a few weeks has gone by since the letter was written, ask the buyer to call their lender for an updated letter.

Ideally, the letter should NOT disclose the buyer's upper limit; you don't want the seller's side to know how much home they can afford to buy because it will hurt their negotiating position. The cover letter should say, "Mr. & Mrs. Buyer are qualified to purchase the house located at 123 Main Street," NOT "Mr. & Mrs. Buyer can purchase a home with a sales price not to exceed $500,000."

Find a mortgage broker who will write letters for you this way. Most are happy to do it since it means they get first crack at the buyer's business. Some, like employees of the big banks, won't have the authority from their company to customize the letter in this way. For me, this is an early warning sign that this lender's pricing is going to be high and their service is going to be slow.

Cover letter

A well-written, professional cover letter can make all the difference in the world. Why? First of all, sellers want to know who is buying their house. It's human nature. Second, it's your opportunity to sell your buyer's credentials and offer things to the sellers that sometimes cost your buyer nothing, like a flexible closing. It allows you the opportunity to show the listing agent that you're a pro and that you can get your client to the closing table on time. And, if your opening offer is a little low, it provides an opportunity for you to explain why. Never, ever, ever present an offer without including a cover letter.

Negotiating Strategies

After your buyer's offer is presented to the seller, he or she has the option to accept your offer, reject your offer, or make a counteroffer. Remember that everything is negotiable, not just the price. In my nineteen years in the industry, I have noticed a few patterns in the way sellers respond to the offers I submit on behalf of my buyer/clients. They include:

The Cave

The Seller accepts the offer with no changes. They agree to the price, closing date, home warranty, title policy, closing costs, etc. This only happens with the most desperate sellers, typically ones who are in danger of losing the home. On deals like these, the seller usually has little or no money to make repairs, so be prepared to buy the house "as is."

Seller Comes Down $1000

This means that they think your buyer's initial offer is ridiculous, but they do want to try to work with you. It is an invitation for them to submit a better offer. This type of response upsets some buyers, which I don't understand. The initial offer gives a lot of information about the seller's circumstances and level of motivation: it means they are not desperate and are not going to give the house away.

Baby Steps

Here, the seller responds to your buyer's offer by dropping $3,000 to $4,000. Your buyer responds by coming up $3,000 to $4000, and so forth. The parties go back and forth until one or the other claims it is his or her final offer, usually after the third round.

Split the difference

Some sellers hate to negotiate and view it as confrontational. These people just want to split the difference and get it over with. I've found that it's usually quite easy to get the seller to reduce their asking price a little more in this scenario, if not with the price, then with other negotiable items like repairs.

What Not to Do

Some buyers are their own worst enemies. Here are some things buyers do during negotiations that cost them money:

Long List of Complaints About the House

As discussed earlier, some unsophisticated buyers like to present the seller with a long list of things that they think are wrong with the house in order to get a better price. This "I'm doing you a favor by buying your home" attitude does nothing but antagonize the seller and creates an unfriendly and risky transaction. If the buyer is making an offer to purchase a property, he or she clearly likes the house and sees value in owning it. If the seller has an opportunity to sell the home to someone more pleasant, they will. And if they don't, they are not going to care for and leave the house in good condition when they leave. Play nice or pay a price.

They Use Their Heart, Not Their Head

The homebuying process is tedious, stressful and, at times, exhausting. There are few decisions greater than this one! By the time the buyer picks a house, they are going to be emotionally invested. This is where you, the agent, need to be the voice of reason for your buyer. Control your buyer's emotions until after repairs have been completed as negotiated, and you are certain it is a good house.

Overpay Out of Fear

There are definitely times when your buyer needs to submit their best offer first, but more often than not there is plenty of room for negotiation. Take an objective look at the seller's situation, the general real estate climate in your area, and at the data that you uncover to see how long it takes similar homes to sell in your area. If the home has a unique feature that can't be found anywhere else, your buyer may need to pay more. If you can find a home similar to this one on any given block, don't submit your best offer right away.

Seller's Response

There are only three ways a seller can respond to an offer. They can accept, reject, or make a counteroffer.

If the Seller Accepts the Contract As-Is

It's rare that the seller accepts the contract with no changes. They almost always counter something. But once in a while it happens, and when it does, the buyer usually gets scared. The buyer wonders if they could have paid less or wonders why the seller is so desperate to sell.

Tell the buyer that some sellers just don't like to negotiate or are in a hurry to make a decision and don't have time to play games. Sometimes the seller's employment company is covering some of the costs, so they really don't care so much about the price. Reassure the buyer that if their inspector finds defects in the property, the inspector will warn the buyer of any potential issues.

If the Seller Counters Some or All of the Terms

If the seller makes a reasonable counteroffer, it's time to strategize. Know what is most important to your buyer. It's usually the price, but it could be closing costs if they are short of cash, the moving date, etc. For example, if your buyer can't qualify for a home priced higher than $200,000, encourage the buyer to agree to the seller's other terms, and just focus on the price.

If the Seller Rejects

Sellers may reject an offer for any number of reasons. They may have a better offer, or they may just be insulted by the offer submitted by your buyer. Find out what the reason is. Usually when they reject, it's because they are insulted, and they are asking the buyer to resubmit an offer at a higher price. It's the seller equivalent of a low-ball offer made by a buyer. Talk to your buyer about submitting a higher offer. Note that this tactic usually angers the buyer, and they often walk away angry, but that's silly. Remind them that it's not personal; it's just how the game is played.

Wrapping It Up

You will go back and forth with the listing agent/seller, until both parties are in agreement to all of the terms. Before final acceptance, confirm all the details with your buyer and do so in writing (email). Then make the changes to the contract and send it to your buyers for their final initials and signatures. Submit the finalized contract to the listing agent ASAP; the listing agent will obtain signatures from the sellers. Both the earnest money check and the option fee need to be delivered to the listing agent and/or title company. Ask the listing agent his or her preference, and try to accommodate them as much as possible.

Once the listing agent receives the checks and final signatures from the sellers, he or she will deliver the executed contract and the earnest money to the title company, if that is your arrangement. The title company will receipt the appropriate pages and email copies to you. If the listing agent has not yet forwarded you a copy of the contract with the seller's signatures, request it from the title company and send a copy to your buyer.

Transaction Management

I've found that the key to a stress-free transaction is transaction management software. Most packages allow you to create a checklist of all the tasks
that need to be completed between now and closing. Each task gets assigned
to the responsible party, and all parties are notified when an item is checked
off the list. A system like this keeps buyers on track, reduces their anxiety,
and minimizes mistakes.

.

Inspections

It is the buyer's job to select an inspector and schedule his or her own inspection. The most that you can do for them is to give them a list of
inspectors that you know do a good job and alert the listing agent of the date
and time the inspector will be there.

Do not attend the inspection. Buyers need time with a neutral party to the
transaction to learn about the quality and condition of the property.

Inspectors have supra keys to access the property and usually deliver their
report to both you and the buyer the same day or the morning after the inspection. It's your job to review the report and recommend to the buyer
which repairs to request. If you and/or the buyer don't understand something
in the report, call the inspector for more information. Inspectors love the opportunity to schmooze Realtors and welcome your call.

Which Repairs to Request

With very, very few exceptions, you should always request that the seller
repair the items in the next section.

Air Conditioner/Heater

If the a/c isn't cooling properly, always request that the seller make the repair prior to closing. In addition, always request that the seller clean the a/c coils, if necessary. Cleaning the coils is not covered by the home warranty since it is a maintenance item. Repairing or replacing the air conditioner is a huge expense that we don't want our buyers to pay.

Roof

Always request that the seller repair or replace the roof prior to closing, based on the findings of the inspector. Keep in mind that the roof has to be insurable, or the buyer won't be able to buy the house; their loan will be denied. If the inspector finds evidence of hail or wind damage, have the seller call their insurance company and file a claim. Sometimes the buyer can get a brand new roof, and it doesn't cost the seller anything other than their deductible.

Termites & Carpenter Ants

If evidence of termites and/or carpenter ants is found, always insist that the seller treat the infestation and repair any damage. Termite treatments should be 'whole house' treatments, not spot treatments. If only one part of the house is sprayed, the termites will simply go underground and reappear on the other side of the house. This should be a non-negotiable item.

Structural Issues

Hopefully your buyer isn't trying to buy a house that has obvious structural damage. However, it is not uncommon for an inspector to point out various little hairline cracks. Their report will either state that the foundation is not in need of repairs or will refer the buyer to a structural engineer. More than half of the time, the referral to the engineer is merely to release the inspector of liability if there is a foundation problem. As Realtors, we can't guarantee the condition of the house, and we have liability issues as well. It's best to recommend that the buyer hire an engineer if they have concerns.

Plumbing

The seller should repair all active water leaks right away to prevent damage to the property. The inspector will make all types of disclosures regarding the plumbing system, and it won't always be obvious which repairs they are recommending. Water heaters, especially when they are located in the attic, are of special concern. If there is a leak, or if it bursts, significant damage can be done to the property. Insist on a replacement or a cash allowance for your buyer to replace the unit, and advise them to replace the unit before they move in. Home warranties will only cover the unit once it breaks; they won't cover any preventive maintenance. Once it breaks, the damage is done.

Electrical

Obviously, all fire hazards need to be repaired. City codes have changed. A house built in the 1980s might not be up to code. It's unrealistic for the seller to rewire the whole house, but it's not unreasonable to expect the electrical system to be safe.

Sprinkler Systems

With the exception of broken sprinkler heads, repairing the sprinkler system can be an expensive proposition. Insist that the seller take care of all issues before closing.

Requesting Repairs

Discuss with your buyer which repairs they would like to request from the seller. Remind your buyer that most sellers are expecting to make at least some repairs, but very few sellers will agree to fix everything. Unless they are buying new construction, they don't get a perfect house.

The repair amendment must be signed and delivered to the listing agent within the option period, and the seller needs time to respond. Try to give the seller at least two days to contemplate repairs, but if, for some reason, this isn't possible (if it was hard to schedule the inspection, for example), discuss extending the option period with the seller's agent.

If the seller agrees to all the repairs, they will sign it and return a copy to you. Assume it's your job to send the repair amendment to the title company. The seller will arrange for repairs to be completed and will be required to deliver receipts prior to closing. Begin requesting repair receipts roughly a week before closing. You and the buyer need time to verify the repairs before closing.

Note: Under no circumstances should you allow your buyer to close if the repairs are not completed to their satisfaction. The contract allows for an extension of the closing date.

Appraisal

Every lender is going to require an appraisal to verify the value of the property. It is important that the appraisal not be ordered until after the inspection is completed and repairs are negotiated. You don't want your buyers to spend $425 on an appraisal if the deal is going to fall apart over repairs or the condition of the house.

Once repairs have been negotiated, you can give the lender permission to order the appraisal. The appraiser has a Supra key to access the property, so agents don't need to be there; they schedule their own appointments through the listing agent or CSS.

The buyer is entitled to a copy of the appraisal. Some lenders forward a copy automatically and others need a reminder. It is important that you and the buyer both receive a copy of the appraisal, since the appraiser measures the house. Compare the square footage on the MLS listing with the square footage reported by the appraiser, and account for any differences.

You also need to ensure that the house appraised for at least the sales price, since a mortgage company will not lend $300,000 to buy a house that is only worth $275,000, for example. This can happen in a seller's market when there is strong demand for housing. Sellers tend to list their home on the high side, and multiple buyers create a bidding war, inflating prices even more.

To protect your buyer from losing their earnest money should a house fail to appraise, we put an appraisal contingency in 'special provisions' of the contract. Contingencies are discussed in an earlier chapter.

Survey

New regulations allow the seller to share their survey with the buyer, as long as there have been no material changes to the property, like the addition of a pool or other permanent structure. If the seller has a survey that they are willing to share, they will send the survey along with an affidavit swearing to the accuracy of the survey to the title company. If a survey is not available or is unacceptable, the title company will order a new one, typically at the buyer's expense unless otherwise specified in the contract.

Financing

The type of financing your buyer secures is as important as the house they choose. I cannot overstate how vital it is for you – as an Exclusive Buyer Agent – to understand the in's and out's of the mortgage industry. The section that follows is the 'in a nutshell' version of how to shop for a loan.

Shopping for a Mortgage

Your buyers need guidance in shopping for a loan. Here are the steps you should tell them to take:

1) Contact four or five lenders and ask for a preliminary quote. It's best to do this on the same day, since interest rates fluctuate daily.
2) Compare the quotes and select the two or three cheapest lenders.
3) Send their top choices the following information:
    a) Full name(s)
    b) Total monthly income(s)

c) Social Security number(s)

d) The property address

e) The loan amount or down payment

f) The property value or sales price

Providing them with this information triggers the requirement that a Loan Estimate (LE) be delivered within three days, but they should request to receive it sooner. The prices quoted on the LE are guaranteed so the lender can't bait and switch the buyer at closing. Some fees can't change more than 10%, and others can't change at all.

After comparing the LEs, select the cheapest loan by looking at the APR. The APR is the cost of the loan after settlement charges have been factored in. The lowest APR wins.

>*Always have the buyer confirm with the lender that they can close on time.*

The big banks (Bank of America, Compass, Wells Fargo and others) generally need at least 45 days to close, often longer. In fact, many listing agents will turn away contracts from banks with reputations for closing late. Most decent mortgage brokers can easily close a loan within 3 to 4 weeks, and their pricing is usually far better than with a bank. You can buy a Wells Fargo loan cheaper through a broker than you can by going directly to Wells Fargo!

>*Buyers should not give these lenders any money or even a credit card number at this point. The lender that they ultimately choose will eventually request payment or a credit card number to guarantee the appraisal. Until then, nobody else gets a dime.*

I included a very detailed document entitled "All About Mortgages" in the appendix section of this book. Read it!

Working with the Lender

The lender will request numerous documents from your buyer. Your job is to do the following:

- Deliver executed copies of the contract and all amendments to the lender as soon as possible.
- Instruct the lender to order the appraisal when the time is right (after repairs are negotiated).
- Check the progress of the loan on a weekly basis; keep the buyer and listing agent up to date.
- Review the appraisal.
- Review the closing statement and verify its accuracy.

Getting to Closing

After the inspection has been completed, repairs have been negotiated, and a lender has been chosen, a lot has to happen before the transaction can close. The following sections discuss this process.

Title Companies

The title company is a neutral third party that manages the transaction after the contract is executed. They also issue the title policy that guarantees the chain of title.

A representative from the title company will first make contact with you when they receive a copy of the contract, usually to send you a receipted copy and to obtain the buyer's lender information. The following sections describe the various title company documents and how you will work with the title company representative.

Title Commitment

Title insurance protects the buyer from a lawsuit that may arise when someone claims an interest in the property. The title commitment is the title company's promise to issue a title policy once certain conditions are met. Doing "title work" means researching the chain of title to verify that the property can legally change hands and that no party other than the seller(s) has an ownership interest.

The title commitment is delivered by the title company to the buyer, lender, seller, and real estate agents of the transaction within 20 days after the Title Company receives a copy of the effective contract. The only page you really need to review is the Schedule C.

Schedule C (Clear in order to Close) is where the title company outlines which requirements must be met in order for the title policy to be issued. If these conditions aren't met, the file can't close, and the deal falls apart. If the seller, for example, has a mortgage/lien against the property, that lien must be paid before the property can legally transfer to the new owners. Other areas of concern are tax liens and judgments. If the IRS has a lien against a house, the seller must have the money to pay off the lien before they can sell. If you notice something of concern on the schedule C, discuss it with the listing agent and title company right away.

Survey

As discussed earlier, if the seller has a survey that they are willing to share, they will deliver it to the title company along with an affidavit, swearing there have been no material changes to the property. The title company will email you and your buyer a copy of the survey and affidavit.

Home Warranty

You need to guide your buyer through the selection process by sending them links to the various companies and reminding them of the amount the seller is willing to pay; the buyer has the option of purchasing additional coverage, if necessary, but any money allocated towards the home warranty that is not spent is wasted.

Once the buyer makes their selection, pass this information along to the title company. The title company will place the order and pay for it at closing.

Schedule Closing

The closing date specified in the contract is the target, but title companies usually won't schedule a closing date/time until they get a "clear to close" and other instructions from the lender. It's not uncommon for closing to be scheduled as late as three or four days before closing.

Closing Statement

The closing statement is prepared by the title company based on the terms of the contract and the instructions from the lender. You will receive a copy and must verify that the buyer received proper credit for the following:

- Option fee
- Earnest money
- Home warranty
- Any repair allowances

Homeowner's Insurance

It is the buyer's responsibility to obtain homeowner's insurance before closing. Homeowner's insurance protects a homeowner against loss from fire and other hazards that may impair the value of their home. It is a lot easier to shop for homeowner's insurance than a mortgage because premiums change only occasionally, so the price they are quoted is very likely the price they will pay.

In shopping for the lowest premium, they need to be very careful to compare apples to apples. Look at two items: the deductible and the coverage.

1) The "deductible" is the loss that is the homeowner's responsibility. Only losses above that amount are insured. Higher deductibles carry lower premiums. But lenders limit the amount of deductible they will allow – one percent is a typical maximum.

2) The "coverage" dictates the maximum loss the policy will pay. There are four levels of coverage:

- Actual cash value (lowest coverage)
- Replacement cost
- Extended replacement cost
- Guaranteed replacement cost (highest coverage, but not necessarily available).

Higher coverage carries higher premiums. Lenders typically require coverage of 125 percent of the cost of replacement, though this may be scaled down if the land accounts for an unusually large percentage of the house value.

Buyers should call several insurance agents for quotes, and when they have made their selections, they should have the insurance agent send a "binder" to the title company. The title company is responsible for collecting money from the buyer and paying for the policy at closing.

Buyer Walk Through

Buyers should always walk through the property 24 to 48 hours before closing to verify repairs and to be certain that the condition of the house is the same as when they last saw it. You should take receipts to the walk through and have them sign an "acceptance of property condition" form.

If the seller fails to repair an item, or if an item has not been repaired to the buyer's satisfaction, contact the listing agent immediately. The contract allows for the contract to be extended if the seller doesn't make the agreed upon repairs, and you should never let the buyer close until all the work has been completed to their satisfaction. If extending the closing date is not an option, negotiate a repair allowance so that the buyers have the cash to make the repair on their own, or have the title company escrow money for the repair.

A lot can happen in the 24 to 48 hours between the walk through and closing. When at all possible, walk through the property immediately before closing to ensure it is still in good condition.

Closing

Once all parties have approved the closing statement (aka Closing Disclosure), it's time to close. Here are the instructions to give to your buyer:

- Get a cashier's check made payable to the title company for the amount 'due from buyer' on page 1 of the Closing Disclosure.
- Bring their driver's license(s) or other form of photo identification to closing.
- On the document entitled Promissory Note, verify that the interest rate and other terms are accurate. This is their promise to pay, and they will be bound by the terms on this document.
- The Truth in Lending document shows the interest rate, annual percentage rate, the amount being financed, and the total cost of the loan over its life. They should definitely give this document a close look to make sure there are no surprises. Remember that the annual percentage rate is NOT the interest rate. It is the true cost of the loan when closing costs are factored in.
- Double check their social security number on the federal tax documents
- The Deed of Trust puts the property up as security for the debt they now owe. Technically, the lender puts a lien on the property. This document is a huge document which explains how the lender will foreclose if the buyer fails to make payments. There

is really nothing to read. This document is promulgated by the state, so the buyer is protected.

- The Monthly Payment document breaks down their monthly mortgage payment showing how much goes to principal, interest, taxes, insurance, and mortgage insurance, if applicable.

Most other documents that are signed at closing are meaningless. The closing agent will explain each document to the buyer as they sign. Your role is very limited. You are really only there in case something unexpected happens and to hold the buyer's hand.

Funding and Keys

Once both the buyer and the seller have signed all the documents, the title company begins the process of funding. Funding is when the seller gets their money; the seller's mortgage is paid off, the home warranty company is paid, and the Realtors get paid. It's also the time when the house "officially" belongs to the buyer. Buyers cannot receive their keys until after funding. No exceptions.

Closing Gifts

I'm not a huge fan of closing gifts, but it's become an expectation in this industry, so I comply. It should be enough, in my opinion, that I've saved my buyers thousands of dollars on their home purchase or that I'm holding their hand through the most important transaction of their lives.

In my opinion, closing gifts diminish the industry. My dentist doesn't send me a gift after my root canal. Lawyers don't buy their clients gifts after they win a big case. The expectation that Realtors buy their clients closing gifts annoys me.

Still, I almost always give them to my full-service buyers, and occasionally give them to my flat-fee buyers. It's been my experience that closing gifts need to be either really memorable or just a small token of thanks; anything in between is a waste of money. Something personalized is usually well received, as are gift cards, but only if they are for $50 or more.

{ 9 }

New Construction, FSBOs & Foreclosures

The information in the previous chapter applied mostly to MLS listed re-sale homes. The following sections will give you information on how to work with Builders, FSBOs, and Foreclosures/Short Sales.

New Construction

There are some advantages to buying a brand new home. First, there is the "new house smell" and the fact that no one else's feet has ever been on the brand new carpet. More importantly, new homes offer energy-saving features unmatched by homes even a few years old. A new home generally has a ten-year structural warranty that includes foundation and load-bearing items, a two-year systems warranty, including electrical, plumbing, and air conditioning, and a one-year floor-to-ceiling warranty. However, for every positive there is a negative and, of course, the negatives range from superficial to deal killer.

For starters, a premium is paid for new construction, and it can take about five years before a new homeowner can build up a decent amount of equity in the house. If they try to sell the house too soon, they will be upside down on their loan. In addition, builders start new communities where there is open land, and that generally means that the commute to work is going to be longer and that the house will be farther away from the center of the city. The biggest risk, however, involves the condition of the house. It may take a year or more before you notice defects in the property. In my area, the risk is caused by our clay-based soil, which leads to a large number of foundation problems. In your area, it may be something different, but the assumption that homes are free of problems simply because they are new is wrong, wrong, wrong.

Types of New Construction

There are three different types of new construction homes: custom homes, spec homes, and tract homes.

Custom Homes

When building a custom home, the buyer makes all the choices. They pick the lot, the builder, the architect, faucets, roof, air conditioning, and everything in between.

On the plus side, they get almost exactly what they want, and they have some control of the price, at least in theory. They move into a home that does not look like every home on the block, and buyers take pride in the fact that they conceptualized their vision and saw it through to fruition.

Now - the down side. The first obstacle is finding a builder that can deliver everything he or she promises. The buyer has to worry about the builder going over budget, running off with the buyer's money, or going bankrupt; whether or not the builder can find quality labor to construct the home; and whether or not the buyer's marriage will survive the process. Chances are the builder will not finish on time, and in the end they will probably only get 95 percent of what they wanted.

Tract Homes

Developers who buy a large piece of land and divide it up into much smaller lots build what are known as "tract" homes. When you think tract home, you might think David Weekley, Meritage Homes, Ryland Homes, First Texas, and others. Generally, the builder has 15 to 20 floor plans that they build in a subdivision, and they are all similar, but not identical. The buyer picks one of the floor plans, chooses the cosmetic items, customizes the floor plan (depending on the builder), and six months later they have a house. Because of the volume of homes being built, and the lower costs of materials and labor, tract homes are generally far less expensive than custom homes. The price and availability are the most appealing things about tract homes. However, you should know that the quality varies not only by builder, but also by area. Do not assume that David Weekley, for example, builds the same quality product in all parts of town. The price point and their desired profit margin most certainly dictate the quality of the materials that they use, and in some areas the quality is horrific.

Spec Homes

A spec home (speculative home for sale) is simply a tract home that is being built without anyone particular in mind. Builders like to have a few homes ready, or almost ready, for buyers who need to move quickly. Sometimes a spec home is available because the original buyer backed out of the transaction for some reason. The same pros and cons that exist for tract homes are true for spec homes.

Buying a Tract or Spec Home

Buying a new tract or spec home is much different from buying a resale home, and buyers find their EBA to be an invaluable asset throughout the process, for the reasons discussed next.

Most builders use their own contract rather than the contract promulgated by the real estate commission in your state, and the contract was not written to be fair. It was written to benefit the builder, not the buyer. And, although it varies by area, most of the salespeople at a builder's model are not Realtors; they work for the builder and are not licensed or regulated by the state. That means that they do not have a legal requirement to treat the buyer fairly, and the only knowledge they have about construction and real estate is what they learn in their builder's training classes. Some builder representatives are better than others, of course. There are some who know a great deal about construction, and others that know much about interior design. The one thing they all have in common, however, is that they want to sell a house. They really don't care if the buyer likes the house, as long as they close and don't say mean things about them online.

Builders welcome, and usually prefer, buyers who are represented by Realtors. Does it cost more to use a Realtor? Sometimes. Most builders say that Realtor commissions come out of their marketing budget so the buyer is not really paying commissions, and I am sure this is true much, but not all, of the time. Generally when builders are selling spec homes, they ask the potential buyer if they have a Realtor before they quote them their best price, and the price is higher if there is a Realtor involved. So what? Buyers begrudge their Realtor the fee they are paid for their expertise; they are there to keep the buyer from getting ripped off! An unrepresented buyer stands to lose a lot more than their Realtor will earn. If they did not have a Realtor, they would have to pay a lawyer, and lawyers don't know very much about buying a home beyond the contracts and title work.

Be sure to advise your buyers to mention to the sales person that they have representation on their first visit. Or, better yet, have them give the builder your business card and tell him to contact you, instead of them. Builder's reps will often tell you things they won't tell the buyers. They don't understand the laws of agency and Exclusive Buyer Representation.

What You Need to Know About New Construction

Spec homes are often listed on the MLS, so you can show them to your buyer just like any other MLS listed home. Builders are most anxious to sell their spec homes first, and here is why: The interest rate for homes under construction (construction financing) is far lower than homes that are finished and move in ready. It is expensive for builders to keep homes in inventory; so spec homes are generally far more negotiable than build jobs, especially if you can close quickly. Here are some more things you should know about new construction:

- Builders do not like to reduce their prices and risk upsetting other buyers who have paid more. You can generally expect a small reduction in price but a large number of "free" upgrades like tile or granite.

- The home your buyers ultimately buy will look nothing like the model. Builders use higher quality materials in their models, and their models are staged to entice buyers. In fact, there is an entire industry dedicated to the cause. I suggest you do not even walk your buyers through the model, unless they are just looking for decorating ideas. Look at one of the builder's spec homes or a build job that is near completion to get a real feel for what the house might look like once it's built. Do not be fooled by their smoke and mirrors.

- The buyer still needs an inspection on a new home. In fact, they need it more since they will be the first person to live in the house.

- If your buyer is building a home, the salesperson will want to write the contract to reflect the sales price plus a detailed list of upgrades, and buyers are expected to decide what they want before they even go to the design center. A better way is to negotiate a dollar amount or a budget to use at the design center.

- When building, be sure to insist on an inspection before the sheetrock goes up to ensure that the space between the studs is clean. It is not uncommon for workers to leave trash and food in the empty house and for garbage and sawdust to be left in between the walls.

- Do not ever, ever, ever buy a home from a builder before researching their reputation online. And buyers shouldn't be afraid to talk to neighbors and find out about their experiences.

- Although new homes come with all kinds of warranties, do not assume the builder is going to honor them, even when they use a third-party warranty company. Warranty companies go out of business all the time, and they have all kinds of "out" clauses that they can use to get out of fixing your house. It is best to pretend that you are buying a resale home (meaning, do your due diligence) and hope you get lucky when you file a warranty claim.

- Builders have preferred lenders and often own their own mortgage companies and title companies. They will offer buyers $5,000 in closing costs, for example, if they use their lender. They claim that their rates are competitive, but buyers must shop around, as they would any other lender. Builders will say they prefer their own lenders because they can control the loan process, but that is not true. Owning a mortgage company is another profit center for the builders. As a buyer, it's all about the math. The cheapest loan, after factoring in the builder's contribution to the closing costs, gets the business. Cost means total cost, not upfront cost. Buyers are losing money if the builder gives them $5,000 in closing costs, but offers them a 4.5 percent interest rate, when they can get 4.25 percent or less through another mortgage company; in the long run, the buyer will save a lot more than $5,000 when they get a loan with a lower interest rate. Don't let your buyers be held hostage by $5,000 and the games builders' play. Most of my buyers find it is cheaper to use their own lenders.

- Builders also offer incentives to use their title company, if they are affiliated with one. The incentive is that they will pay for the buyer's title policy. If the title incentive is separate from the mortgage incentive, it can be a pretty good deal. But, as always, it's all about the math.

Representing Your Buyer

Assuming the builder is reputable, representing a buyer in the purchase of a new home can be easier than helping them buy a resale home. The onsite sales consultant writes the contract and facilitates the transaction. You are simply there to ensure the buyer doesn't get bamboozled. The builder is going to convince someone to buy the house that backs up to the grocery story or the railroad tracks; don't let it be your buyer.

Most buyers don't realize the extent to which the builder stacks the deck against them. The following are some things you need to know to protect your buyer:

- When your buyer purchases a home through a builder, the buyer uses their own contract, which was written by their lawyers, not your state real estate commission, as is the case with a resale home (in most states). You can't interpret the contract for the buyer, but you must ensure that the buyer understands what is required of them. Get a copy of the contract and take your client out for a cup of coffee. Read the contract together, and be sure that they know what commitments they are making. Do NOT let them sign it before they read and understand the entire document. Read it to them if you have to.

- The onsite salesperson has permission from the builder to offer buyers certain concessions in the form of price reductions and upgrades. Buyer requests beyond their allowance must be submitted to their manager for approval.

- Take your buyer to see a builder spec home, but spend very little time exploring the model. Most models are loaded with upgrades and are designed to entice and trick the buyer. Their home will not be of the same quality or have the same decorator features.

- When your buyer has decided to purchase new construction, the onsite rep writes an offer and presents it to their manager for a signature. They encourage the buyer to submit an offer that may include a reduction of price and a variety of upgrades like blinds, upgraded granite, etc. I prefer to ask for a specific upgrade allowance. The buyer has no idea what they want until they get to the design center and view their options

- If you are helping a buyer build a home, encourage them to have the builder install several electrical outlets around the roofline/perimeter of the house for Christmas lights. Also, when installing a sprinkler system, have one zone specifically to control soaker hoses so that the foundation can be watered independently of the grass.

- Builders have their own contracts and procedures. It's wise to visit the builders in your area to become familiar with their product and policies, and to develop a relationship with their onsite personnel.

Foreclosures and Short Sales

When a homeowner stops making his or her mortgage payment, the bank takes back the house in a process called foreclosure. A short sale is a house that sells for less than the balance on its mortgage. Banks must approve short sales, and it is typically in their best interest to do so since they will recoup more money than they would if the house went into foreclosure.

The techniques to buy property that has been foreclosed upon, and the risks involved in doing so, are beyond the scope of this book. In fact, I generally stay out of the foreclosure market. My experience with foreclosures has demonstrated to me that it is difficult to make the math work. Let's say there is a bank-owned property (foreclosure) that is listed for $200,000. You estimate that the home needs roughly $35,000 worth of repairs and improvements. You analyze the market and determine that homes of similar size in good condition sell for an average of $245,000. Assuming there are no unexpected surprises, you could fix up the house and make a $10,000 profit. Is $10,000 enough to justify the substantial risk and effort involved with buying properties that are typically in poor condition? To some, it is. It was to me when I first started flipping homes. I soon realized I was making below minimum wage for my efforts and learned that I had to start buying homes cheaper if I was going to make a living as a flipper.

It is very, very difficult, in my opinion, to buy a foreclosed house cheap enough to make it worth the trouble and to justify the risk. The only exception I have found involves very high-end luxury homes. So, I don't recommend that you jump into the foreclosure market. There are plenty of dumpy homes on the market that are priced to sell; encourage your buyers to buy one of those instead.

Homeowners who are in financial distress are much more motivated to unload their property than is a bank.

Short sales can be worth pursuing under certain circumstances. The problem, however, is that the bank can take months to approve the contract. If you are looking at short sales, focus on the ones that already have bank approval, and save yourself weeks of not knowing if your buyer is going to be able to buy a particular house.

For Sale By Owner (FSBOs)

FSBOs are homes being marketed without the help of an agent; they are not always listed on the MLS, but you can still help a buyer purchase a home that is for sale by owner. A home is for sale by owner for one of these reasons:

- The homeowners hate Realtors.
- The homeowners think they can do a lot of what a seller's agent does on their own, without paying a six percent commission.
- The homeowners do not have enough equity in the home to pay Realtor fees, so they have no choice but to sell it themselves.

FSBOs have more options than ever when it comes to selling their homes. In the past, in order to get their home listed on the MLS, homeowners had no choice but to hire a Realtor to represent them and pay a five to seven percent commission.

These days, they can pay $200 to $500 and have their home listed on the MLS. Once listed, every Realtor in that area can view the listing and show the home to prospective buyers. The seller offers a commission to the Realtor that brings the buyer, and they pay about half of what they normally would in commissions. This is a very smart way to sell a home, in my opinion, as long as they make it easy for Realtors to show the house.

I hate, hate, hate working with FSBOs!!

Why? Homeowners typically do not know how to value their property and the home is often priced incorrectly. I love finding a great house for sale by owner that is priced far too low, and it thrills me when my clients get a great deal. But, more often than not, the house is overpriced and working with the seller is difficult at best. I work with FSBOs all the time, but I hate it. Most will not use a lockbox, making it necessary for the seller to provide access to the property. That means I have to make an appointment with the seller directly, versus one call to a service that makes all my appointments for me. When I call the owner to schedule an appointment, they are always suspicious of me and generally grumpy because so many listing agents have contacted them trying to list their home. The seller insists on showing us around the house and it is awkward, since most buyers do not feel comfortable opening doors and looking in closets when the seller is present. The showing takes three times longer than usual because the seller wants to make small talk and woo the buyers. In addition, the homes are seldom worth considering because they did not have a Realtor advising them on the best way to present their home to buyers. Yes, I hate working with FSBOs.

Still, I always look for FSBOs for my clients, but not right away. Once I have a really good idea of what my buyers are looking for and where, I preview by owner homes and only take my clients to see the strong possibilities. I also do a quick Comparative Market Analysis (CMA) to see how the home is priced, and I try to get as much information about the seller and the house as possible in case my client decides to make an offer. The seller needs to have an idea of how real estate is sold in my state because I'm not their representative, and it is not my job to help the homeowner sell the house. I will not let my buyers spend a dime until I am convinced that the seller will actually close the deal. After all, the seller has nothing to lose. My buyer pays for inspections and appraisals, and they will lose hundreds of dollars if the seller does not close. It is my job to ensure that does not happen. Your buyer needs to understand all of these things about FSBOs lest they accuse you of being lazy or assume that you are trying to hide something from them. Sometimes you are protecting them from a seller who has no idea what they are doing.

{ 10 }

Final Words

Buying and selling real estate is complicated! You won't feel 100% comfortable with the process until you've completed at least five transactions. Even then, each deal is different, each house is different, and you're dealing with different personalities, ranging from angel to lunatic. As you venture out on your own, remember the following:

- Never, ever lie or even guess. If you're not sure about your answer, tell your buyer you'll find out and get back to them. And do! They will respect you for not playing the PIDOOMA game.
- Don't gossip or speak badly about other Realtors. Listing agents have the listings, and you'll want them to sell those listings to your buyers. Be friendly and professional, but don't make them your buddy.
- Don't be in the business of pursuing another agent's buyer. If they come to you seeking representation, help them dissolve their relationship with their former agent and then happily repre-

sent them. Other agents might try to steal your buyers; you have more integrity than that.

- You're going to make mistakes…I guarantee it. Don't try to hide the mistake; your buyer's money is on the line. Make it right and move on. If that means paying for a repair or an inspection, do it.

- Treat every homebuyer like they are your little brother or little sister. Do the right thing for them…always.

- If your buyer is making a mistake, tell them. Even if you hate them and can't wait for them to close and go away, express your concern and let them make their own decision. That's part of 'doing the right thing.'

- Don't let buyers abuse you. An occasional last minute showing can be accommodated, but not as a general rule. You get to have a career in real estate and have a life.

- Don't over reach. Let the loan officer do his or her job. You don't need to know everything there is to know about title insurance. There is usually a minimum of 13 professionals involved in any given real estate transaction. Know where your job ends and the next guy's job begins.

- Ignore, ignore, ignore the noise from other agents! I still struggle with this one, even after all these years. Others will criticize your business model, or tell you you're wrong for not working with sellers since, in theory, you're cutting your income in half. It's really not true. What you're doing is offering something unique that is in demand. You're taking yourself away from the herd. Most Realtors make about $25,000 to $35,000 a year! They have no business giving you advice.

Mistakes New Agents Make

Realtors inevitably make mistakes, especially new Realtors. It's hard to decipher the good advice from the bad, and it seems everyone has their hands in your pocket. The following are some common mistakes new agents make right out of the gate.

They Buy Far More Than They Need

I used to love the start of a new school year. It was so much fun to buy new pencils, notebooks, and backpacks, and I loved organizing all my new supplies and placing them neatly in my locker. So exciting!

Your first year in real estate is kind of like that. Everything is shiny and new, and you can't wait to surround yourself with all the "stuff" that is going to help you launch your new career.

Realtors are bombarded on a regular basis by companies selling printing, pens, signs, insurance, software, websites, advertising, computers, training manuals, seminars, cars, pictures, mailing lists, brochure boxes, key cabinets, info tubes, lockboxes, computers, printers, phones, etc. Combine these with board dues and desk fees, and a Realtor can go bankrupt in a hurry!

The truth is that you need a lot less than you think to get started! Spend your money wisely! Buying custom pens and Frisbees isn't going to make you any money. Your picture on a grocery cart? Not so much in the short-term. A decent website? Definitely.

They Rely on the Broker For Prospects and Business

As we discussed earlier, there was a time when you could count on your broker to generate enough leads to keep you in business. But the business has changed. Brokers take a 35 to 40% cut vs. a 50% cut. There are 100% commission programs. And you have to generate your own leads or perish.

They Don't Pre-Qualify Buyers Before Putting Them in the Car

I have yet to meet a Realtor who hasn't made this mistake. In our excitement to launch our career, we'll toss anyone in the car and start driving them around town. We'll show them houses without first confirming that they are ready, willing, and able to buy a home!

Don't spend your time and gas on people who are not ready, willing, and able to buy a home!

You will take very good care of your clients, I'm sure. But be certain they can actually qualify for a loan before you spend a significant amount of time with them. Know that they are willing to pull the trigger once they find the right house. Don't show them homes in January when their lease doesn't expire until April (unless they are willing to break their lease). It's desperate. Don't ever position yourself as a desperate agent.

They Don't Enter the Business with Enough Money

Any time you start your own business, you need funds to sustain yourself. Business cards are a one time, small expense, at least initially. But board fees, desk fees, and marketing expenses happen each and every month. Know how you're going to support yourself initially. Plan on working for about 3 to 4 months with no income.

They Assume Their Family & Friends Will Hire Them

Ah, the myths of the sphere of influence; the misconception that you can go into real estate, tell all your friends and family, and you will have business in an instant.

Here's why it doesn't work. First of all, no one wants to refer their friends to you when you're a brand new agent. You have no track record, and you're still pronouncing "Realtor" like "Real a tor." Stop that, by the way. Second, your friends and family don't always want you to know about their finances, credit, buying power, etc. Some things are private.

> *The truth about your sphere of influence is this: If your friends and family use you to buy or sell a house, they are going to expect you to do it for free.*

If you're entering the business assuming your sphere of influence will help you launch your career, you're in for a big, big surprise! They'll use you and abuse you, and you'll never get a single client from them. Once you've proven yourself for a couple of years, you might see some business from them, but not when you're a newbie.

First Steps

If you're a broker, getting started is easy. Declare yourself an Exclusive Buyer Agent and develop your marketing plan.

If you're new to the business, contact an Exclusive Buyer's Agency in your area and see if they will sponsor you. Some may be resistant to the flat-fee model; see what you can negotiate.

If you live in Texas, or if you can't find an EBA to sponsor you in your state, give me a call. HelpUBuy America is rapidly expanding across the state of Texas and across the country. I might be interested in opening an office in your area.

Please feel free to contact me with any questions or comments about the information in this book. I'm happy to help you launch your career in any way that I can.

About the Author

 Alysse Musgrave is a graduate of Texas A&M University and has been a licensed real estate broker in the state of Texas since 1995. While working as a systems analyst, she developed an interest in flipping houses and earned her real estate license to support her personal investment efforts.

Learning firsthand of the pitfalls and negative aspects of buying and selling real estate, Alysse developed an empathy for others who experienced her frustration. Especially discouraged by the lack of representation she received as a buyer, Alysse decided the time was right to bring Exclusive Buyer Agency to the Dallas/Ft. Worth area, and she opened what would become one of the country's oldest and most successful exclusive buyer brokerages.

HelpUBuyAmerica.com is an Exclusive Buyer Agency whose mission it is to protect the rights of homebuyers in Austin, Houston, and Dallas.

{Appendix 1}

All About Mortgages

I started talking about predatory lending and improper homebuying practices over 20 years ago. I received a lot of hate mail and even anonymous threats from mortgage 'professionals' (aka mob bosses) who did not want their secrets revealed.

> *Today, lenders are required to be far more transparent in their pricing and loan programs. While it's still very possible to rip off an uneducated, unprepared borrower, mortgage law makes it much harder to rip off someone who knows how the system works.*

I spend a lot of time educating my buyers before we ever really talk seriously about buying. The following pages are intended to "give it to you in a nutshell." Education is vital if we are going to eliminate predatory lending practices. Let's get started.

Some Definitions

Mortgage brokers hire loan officers to sell loans to consumers. They have accounts with wholesale lenders, who are the actual source of the funds. Each day, the wholesale lenders will provide the mortgage brokers, and all their loan officers, with wholesale rate sheets. The mortgage broker decides how much profit he or she wants to make on each loan and creates a retail rate sheet. The loan officers sell from the retail rate sheet. The difference between the wholesale rate, the retail rate, and the closing fees makes up the lender's profit margin.

Mortgage Brokers vs. Banks

When shopping for a loan, a buyer can use a mortgage broker or deal directly with the bank. What follows is a simplification of the differences between the two.

Mortgage Brokers

A mortgage broker is extremely knowledgeable in the field of mortgages. They know the market and keep track of which lender might be offering a discount or have a unique product. When a buyer works with a broker, the broker compares wholesale mortgage rates from all kinds of banks and lending institutions; they can often get a better price than if a buyer went to the bank directly. It's not uncommon for a broker to sell a Wells Fargo loan, for example, at a lower price than a buyer could get if he/she went directly to Wells Fargo! Because there is less bureaucracy with a mortgage broker, the process is generally more streamlined and efficient (assuming an equal level of competency). Mortgage brokers are *required* to disclose to the buyer their commission (called a Yield Spread Premium), so the buyer will always know the profit the broker is making on the loan.

A good mortgage broker is worth his or her weight in gold. A bad one, well...

Banks

Bank of America, Wells Fargo, and Chase are examples of big banks that can loan money to buy a house. These banks have the capital to permanently keep a mortgage in their portfolio. The buyer gets a mortgage through Chase and makes his/her payments to Chase until the loan is paid off.

Smaller, regional banks don't have the long-term funds available to keep loans for very long. They issue mortgages that conform to industry standards and sell them to investors almost immediately, locking in their profits.

Banks differ from brokers in that they don't have to disclose their profits (Yield Spread Premium) to the borrower. It's the goal of many brokers to meet the qualifications necessary to call them-selves a bank so they can avoid this disclosure requirement. YSPs are a controversial topic in the industry.

Big banks are known for being inefficient and expensive. In my area, many listing agents advise their seller/clients *not* to accept a buyer's contract when their lender comes from one of these institutions, and I agree with their rea-soning. While a small bank or a broker can close a transaction in 3 or 4 weeks, the big banks often take 6 weeks or longer, and they still often miss the closing date. Their loan officers tend to be untrained order takers who are not really qualified to offer financial advice to buyers. The loan files move – slowly and inaccurately – from department to department. Dealing with the big banks adds an unnecessary layer of stress to the transaction.

Loan officers that work for brokers or small banks are far more knowledgeable and service-oriented; I have someone to call if there's a problem that needs to be resolved. The same isn't true with a big bank.

Do yourself a favor. Advise your clients to stick with a small, regional bank or a broker. You'll be glad you did.

How Lenders Make Money

Mortgage brokers make money several different ways. They can manipulate these potential profit avenues all day long to come up with their desired profit. The following sections describe the various ways mortgage brokers make money.

Closing costs

This includes fees for applications, credit reports, appraisals, processing, underwriting, document preparation, and so forth. These fees are sometimes referred to as "junk fees."

Origination fees

Origination fees are usually one percent of the loan amount. This is simply a fee that the broker charges for writing the loan.

Discount Points

Points are prepaid interest. They are usually only charged when the buyer wants an interest rate that is below market rates. Discount points are expressed as a percentage of the loan amount. One point is equal to one percent of the loan amount, three points is equal to three percent of the loan amount, and so forth. Example: If the buyer is quoted an interest rate of 7.25 percent with zero points, but they have their heart set on an interest rate of seven percent, they could pay one point and buy the interest rate down to this amount.

Yield Spread Premiums (YSPs)

YSPs are rebates paid by wholesale lenders to mortgage brokers for writing loans that are above "par" or market interest rates. If the par rate is eight percent, but the mortgage broker can get the buyer to pay 8.5 percent, the wholesale lender will pay the broker an extra commission called a Yield Spread Premium. YSPs can help consumers who are short on cash. They can pay a higher interest rate and have their mortgage broker pay some of their closing costs. There is nothing inherently wrong with a YSP, unless it is used for improper purposes.

How Your Client Can Get Ripped Off

Closing costs

Some closing costs are legitimate fees for services performed by a third party. The buyer's credit report and appraisal are examples of legitimate fees - some of these fees are collected upfront. Some legitimate fees (like processing fees) are collected at closing. Are all other fees junk fees? It is impossible to say. There are an endless number of ways that lenders can manipulate closing costs. They can waive most of the closing costs and charge a higher interest rate. The borrower still pays, of course; they simply do not pay upfront. Lenders can charge for services that are never performed. They can charge $400 for an appraisal that costs $250.

Origination Fee

There are legitimate costs associated with loan origination, and the lender is entitled to make a fair profit. To charge a one percent origination is fine, but to charge a one percent origination fee in conjunction with inflated or fabricated closing costs and premium interest rates could be considered excessive.

Discount points

Discount points are points paid for their stated purpose. Reducing the consumer's interest rate is a good purpose, but a dishonest lender can quote a certain rate at the time of the loan application and produce something quite different at the closing table. For example, your buyer may be told that because of a past credit problem the do not qualify for the best rate. They are "forced" to either buy down the interest rate by paying additional discount points or agree to a higher rate, in which case the broker receives a rebate in the form of a Yield Spread Premium, which is discussed next.

Yield Spread Premiums

If the loan officer can get your buyer to pay a higher-than-market interest rate, they get a "rebate" called a Yield Spread Premium. This is how it happens. The buyer agrees to a 30-year loan at 6.5 percent. Since interest rates change daily, their loan officer will not lock in the interest rate right away. They will "float' the loan until there is a little dip in rates, and then they will lock in the loan - let's say at 6.25 percent.

Since the loan officer has your buyer committed to pay 6.5 percent, he or she will get an extra commission for selling a loan at a higher-than-market interest rate. These commissions are often in the multiple thousands! An upfront and ethical loan officer would have rebated the borrower the YSP or given them the 6.25 percent interest rate.

Since the lender (brokers only) is not required to disclose this extra profit to the borrower until closing, the borrower is none the wiser until it is too late to do anything about it. YSPs provide a useful option to some borrowers. For those with little cash, YSPs make no-cost mortgages possible because the lender pays closing costs. For those who expect to be in their house only a few years, YSPs permit a favorable exchange of higher rate for lower fees. However, in the hands of unscrupulous lenders, they can cost the borrower thousands and thousands of dollars.

How Can All This Happen?

Mortgage brokers are regulated by RESPA and other state agencies, and the good news is that highly positive changes have been made in the past few years. Lenders can no longer charge more than 3% in fees, and disclosures made to the borrower are more meaningful and easier to understand. Most closing costs can no longer increase by more than 10%; the lender is required to rebate any excess overages back to the borrower at closing. They can't pull a "bait and switch" by offering one interest rate upfront and raising it at the closing table (now they can do it 3 days before closing, as you'll read later). But it can still be tough to enforce the rules, so fraud still exists. Anxious, emotional homebuyers are very easy to manipulate. The best thing you can do as a Realtor is to educate your buyer.

The Lender's Dilemma

Interest rates are based on risk; the better the buyer's credentials, the lower their interest rate. Because it is a risk-based system, the borrower will not learn their final interest rate until after they make a formal loan application and until the lender locks the rate. It's a "chicken or the egg" scenario. Lenders don't want to commit to pricing until the buyer makes a formal loan application, and buyers don't want to commit to a loan without knowing the costs.

Closing costs are disclosed to borrowers on a document called a Loan Estimate (LE).

There was a time when a lender could provide a potential borrower a Good Faith Estimate (now known as a Loan Estimate) and it was understood that the figures were just estimates. But beginning in 2010, the lender is bound by most of the fees that they quote. As such, many lenders now provide an "Initial Fees Worksheet" or a "Financing Scenario" while the borrower shops for a mortgage, instead of a Loan Estimate which commits them to the prices that they quote.

By giving the borrower this document, the lender is giving them a price without actually making a commitment.

So what does this all mean? It means that the Department of Housing and Urban Development's (HUD) recent initiatives to make shopping for a loan easier for buyers have failed, and borrowers are still going to have to take extra steps to avoid being ripped off.

A lender is not necessarily a crook simply because they give a buyer an Initial Fees Worksheet instead of an LE; this is the policy of some of the most honest and competent lenders I know. It's a matter of practicality and risk reduction.

However, it is a manipulation of the system, and the system doesn't make it easy for borrowers to tell the difference between the good guys and the bad guys. Advise your buyers to follow the procedures discussed later to ensure they won't be ripped off.

Qualified Mortgages & Ability to Repay

Lenders are now encouraged to ensure that borrowers have the ability to repay their mortgages. In return, lenders will be protected from borrower lawsuits so long as they issue "safe" mortgages that follow guidelines. Certain loans are not allowed, including the following:

- Interest-only loans
- Negative amortization
- Large balloon payments
- Loans that are longer than 30 years
- Excessive upfront points & fees
- A debt to income ration of more than 43%

As the Consumer Financial Protection Bureau (CFPB) website puts it: "The ability-to-repay rule is intended to prevent consumers from getting trapped in mortgages that they cannot afford, and to prevent lenders from making loans that consumers do not have the ability to repay. It's that simple." Enough said.

How to Find a Lender

Chances are you have heard that the best place to find a lender is through a friend or family member. I disagree. Friends and family probably have no idea if they were ripped off, and unless they work in the industry, they are no match for a predatory lender. Some say that the agent is not a good resource; again, I disagree. You will quickly learn which lenders can close on time, which lenders deliver what they promise, and which lenders treat customers fairly. The lenders that we, as agents, recommend should be those that go out of their way to treat our buyers well so we will continue to send them clients. Provide your buyers with a list of your favorite agents and advise them to give them all a call, but also remind your buyers that they are not required to use any vendor that you, their Realtor, recommend.

Loan Estimate Form

The Consumer Financial Protection Bureau (CFPB) requires easy-to-understand mortgage disclosure forms that clearly lay out the terms of a mortgage for a homebuyer. The new "Know Before You Owe" mortgage forms known as the Loan Estimate (LE) and the Closing Disclosure (CD) replaced the Good Faith Estimate (GFE) and HUD-1 in October 2015. These new forms help consumers understand their options, choose the deal that is best for them, and avoid costly surprises at the closing table.

Shopping for a Loan

After your buyer has found a house, they should contact several lenders and ask for quotes. The loan officer will either refer them to the loan company's online loan application site or take information from the buyer over the phone, and then send them either a Loan Estimate or an Initial Fees Worksheet. Your buyer should compare the documents, with your help if needed, and pursue the least expensive ones *that can close on time.*

Remember, if the pricing isn't given to the borrower on a Loan Estimate form, it can change.

THIS STEP IS IMPORTANT

Your buyer should send to their top choices the following information. Do so in writing (email is fine) with a return receipt:

- Full name(s)
- Monthly income(s)
- Social Security number(s)
- The property address
- The loan amount
- The property value or sales price

Providing the lenders with *all* of this information triggers the requirement that a Loan Estimate be delivered *within three days*. The lender is required by RESPA (mortgage law) to give the borrower a Loan Estimate and all the price guarantees that come along with it. Changes in income, sales price, loan program, or locking the interest rate can trigger a new Loan Estimate, rendering the original one obsolete. The final Loan Estimate is the one that must match the settlement statement at closing.

After comparing several Loan Estimates, your buyer should select the best loan for them and notify the loan originator that they would like to proceed with the loan. Advise them to keep their original Loan Estimate so they can compare it with the final settlement costs stated on the Closing Disclosure (discussed later), even though the Closing Disclosure includes a comparison of what was quoted and what was delivered. Some charges cannot be raised, and the lender must reimburse the borrower if those charges were illegally or erroneously increased. Others can go up by a ten percent margin, and the lender has to reimburse the borrower for any excess.

The loan officer may want your buyer to give him a credit card number or a check so that he can order the appraisal. Advise your buyer to NOT give them a dime until they are 100 percent certain that they plan to use that lender. BORROWERS ARE NOT RE-QUIRED TO USE A LENDER SIMPLY BECAUSE THEY RECEIVED A LOAN ESTIMATE.

The new Loan Estimate document is so well written that it needs no explanation. Really. The Loan Estimate is three pages long. The first page contains information identifying the borrower and loan, the loan terms, the projected monthly payments, the total estimated closing costs, and the total estimated cash needed to close. The second page breaks down the closing costs in more detail and includes information on prepaid and escrowed amounts, as well as detail on the cash needed to close. The third page includes a summary of loan costs over five years (to provide for a comparison with other loan products), along with required disclosures regarding the delivery of a copy of an appraisal to the borrower, whether the loan is assumable, whether homeowner's insurance is required, late payment fee information, and whether the loan servicing may be transferred. The third page also contains a signature block for consumers to confirm receipt of the disclosure.

4321 Random Boulevard • Somecity, ST 12340

Save this Loan Estimate to compare with your Closing Disclosure.

Loan Estimate

DATE ISSUED	2/15/2013	LOAN TERM	30 years
		PURPOSE	Purchase
		PRODUCT	Fixed Rate
APPLICANTS	Michael Jones and Mary Stone	LOAN TYPE	☒ Conventional ☐FHA ☐VA ☐ ___
	123 Anywhere Street	LOAN ID #	123456789
	Anytown, ST 12345	RATE LOCK	☐ NO ☒ YES, until 4/16/2013 at 5:00 p.m. EDT
PROPERTY	456 Somewhere Avenue		*Before closing, your interest rate, points, and lender credits can*
	Anytown, ST 12345		*change unless you lock the interest rate. All other estimated*
SALE PRICE	$180,000		*closing costs expire on 3/4/2013 at 5:00 p.m. EDT*

Loan Terms		Can this amount increase after closing?	
Loan Amount	$162,000	NO	
Interest Rate	3.875%	NO	
Monthly Principal & Interest *See Projected Payments below for your Estimated Total Monthly Payment*	$761.78	NO	
		Does the loan have these features?	
Prepayment Penalty		YES	• As high as $3,240 if you pay off the loan during the first 2 years
Balloon Payment		NO	

LOAN ESTIMATE - TOP OF PAGE ONE

Projected Payments

Payment Calculation	Years 1-7	Years 8-30
Principal & Interest	$761.78	$761.78
Mortgage Insurance	+ 82	+ —
Estimated Escrow *Amount can increase over time*	+ 206	+ 206
Estimated Total Monthly Payment	**$1,050**	**$968**

		This estimate includes	In escrow?
Estimated Taxes, Insurance & Assessments *Amount can increase over time*	**$206** a month	[X] Property Taxes [X] Homeowner's Insurance [ ] Other: *See Section G on page 2 for escrowed property costs. You must pay for other property costs separately.*	YES YES

Costs at Closing

Estimated Closing Costs	**$8,054**	Includes $5,672 in Loan Costs + $2,382 in Other Costs – $0 in Lender Credits. *See page 2 for details.*
Estimated Cash to Close	**$16,054**	Includes Closing Costs. *See Calculating Cash to Close on page 2 for details.*

Visit **www.consumerfinance.gov/mortgage-estimate** for general information and tools.

LOAN ESTIMATE   PAGE 1 OF 3 · LOAN ID # 123456789

LOAN ESTIMATE - BOTTOM OF PAGE ONE

Closing Cost Details

Loan Costs

A. Origination Charges	$1,802
.25 % of Loan Amount (Points)	$405
Application Fee	$300
Underwriting Fee	$1,097

B. Services You Cannot Shop For	$672
Appraisal Fee	$405
Credit Report Fee	$30
Flood Determination Fee	$20
Flood Monitoring Fee	$32
Tax Monitoring Fee	$75
Tax Status Research Fee	$110

Other Costs

E. Taxes and Other Government Fees	$85
Recording Fees and Other Taxes	$85
Transfer Taxes	

F. Prepaids	$867
Homeowner's Insurance Premium (6 months)	$605
Mortgage Insurance Premium (months)	
Prepaid Interest ($17.44 per day for 15 days @ 3.875%)	$262
Property Taxes (months)	

G. Initial Escrow Payment at Closing		$413
Homeowner's Insurance $100.83 per month for 2 mo.		$202
Mortgage Insurance per month for mo.		
Property Taxes $105.30 per month for 2 mo.		$211

H. Other	$1,017
Title – Owner's Title Policy (optional)	$1,017

I. TOTAL OTHER COSTS (E + F + G + H)	$2,382

LOAN ESTIMATE - TOP OF PAGE TWO

C. Services You Can Shop For	$3,198
Pest Inspection Fee	$135
Survey Fee	$65
Title – Insurance Binder	$700
Title – Lender's Title Policy	$535
Title – Settlement Agent Fee	$502
Title – Title Search	$1,261
D. TOTAL LOAN COSTS (A + B + C)	**$5,672**

J. TOTAL CLOSING COSTS	$8,054
D + I	$8,054
Lender Credits	

Calculating Cash to Close

Total Closing Costs (J)	$8,054
Closing Costs Financed (Paid from your Loan Amount)	$0
Down Payment/Funds from Borrower	$18,000
Deposit	– $10,000
Funds for Borrower	$0
Seller Credits	$0
Adjustments and Other Credits	$0
Estimated Cash to Close	**$16,054**

LOAN ESTIMATE - BOTTOM OF PAGE TWO

Additional Information About This Loan

LENDER	Ficus Bank
NMLS/__ LICENSE ID	
LOAN OFFICER	Joe Smith
NMLS/__ LICENSE ID	12345
EMAIL	joesmith@ficusbank.com
PHONE	123-456-7890

MORTGAGE BROKER	
NMLS/__ LICENSE ID	
LOAN OFFICER	
NMLS/__ LICENSE ID	
EMAIL	
PHONE	

Comparisons — Use these measures to compare this loan with other loans.

In 5 Years	$56,582	Total you will have paid in principal, interest, mortgage insurance, and loan costs.
	$15,773	Principal you will have paid off.
Annual Percentage Rate (APR)	4.274%	Your costs over the loan term expressed as a rate. This is not your interest rate.
Total Interest Percentage (TIP)	69.45%	The total amount of interest that you will pay over the loan term as a percentage of your loan amount.

LOAN ESTIMATE - TOP OF PAGE THREE 1

206

Other Considerations

Appraisal	We may order an appraisal to determine the property's value and charge you for this appraisal. We will promptly give you a copy of any appraisal, even if your loan does not close. You can pay for an additional appraisal for your own use at your own cost.
Assumption	If you sell or transfer this property to another person, we ☐ will allow, under certain conditions, this person to assume this loan on the original terms. ☒ will not allow assumption of this loan on the original terms.
Homeowner's Insurance	This loan requires homeowner's insurance on the property, which you may obtain from a company of your choice that we find acceptable.
Late Payment	If your payment is more than *15* days late, we will charge a late fee of *5% of the monthly principal and interest payment.*
Refinance	Refinancing this loan will depend on your future financial situation, the property value, and market conditions. You may not be able to refinance this loan.
Servicing	We intend ☐ to service your loan. If so, you will make your payments to us. ☒ to transfer servicing of your loan.

Confirm Receipt

By signing, you are only confirming that you have received this form. You do not have to accept this loan because you have signed or received this form.

Applicant Signature	Date	Co-Applicant Signature	Date

LOAN ESTIMATE - BOTTOM OF PAGE THREE

Types of Loans

Over the past few years, subprime and no money down financing programs have disappeared, and the mortgage industry has gone back to traditional mortgage programs. FHA and Conventional financing are the most traditional type of financing.

If your buyer can qualify for conventional financing, it is the least expensive option. If not, they can pursue an FHA. Some people mistakenly believe that FHA loans are strictly for low-income borrowers. This is absolutely not true. People of all incomes obtain FHA loans.

The following sections highlight the requirements and benefits of each type of loan.

Conventional vs. FHA Financing

FHA Financing

FHA is a government-insured mortgage program, meaning the government guarantees the loan if the borrower defaults. This type of financing was part of the government's initiative to encourage homeownership. The credit requirements are much more relaxed, and borrowers can often get a loan with a 580 credit score. The minimum down payment on an FHA loan is 3.5 percent of the purchase price, and they *do* accept gifted funds from a close relative.

The FHA program is becoming more and more popular lately, since it is easier to qualify for than a conventional mortgage. FHA is, however, more expensive than conventional financing.

Mortgage Insurance Premium (MIP)

Mortgage insurance is an insurance policy that protects lenders in the event a borrower defaults on the loan. FHA loans require two different types of mortgage insurance premiums for most buyers. The first is called the Upfront Mortgage Insurance Premium (UFMIP), and is a percentage (approximately 1.5 percent) of the total amount being borrowed. It can be paid in cash at closing or can be rolled into the loan amount. The second type of mortgage insurance is called monthly MIP (Mortgage Insurance Premium). MIP premiums are paid as part of the monthly mortgage payments. In years past, MIP could be cancelled once the borrower had roughly 20% equity in the home, either through appreciation or principal reduction. *Those days are gone.* In 2013 the rules changed. FHA borrowers who put less than 10% down will have to pay the MIP premium for the life of the loan. I'll repeat this statement for emphasis.

> *FHA borrowers who put down less than 10% will have to pay the annual MIP for the life of the loan.*

If your buyer has a credit score of 680 or higher, but little money in the bank, a better loan for them is the Conventional 97, discussed later.

Conventional Financing

A conventional loan is a loan that is not insured by the government; the lender takes on the risk of losing money in the event that the borrower defaults on the mortgage. Conventional mortgages are for those borrowers with better credit; credit scores need to be in the 680 plus range. Borrowers can expect to put down between 3 percent and 20 percent when they purchase a home using a conventional mortgage.

Private Mortgage Insurance (PMI)

Most lenders require private mortgage insurance (PMI) when the buyer puts down less than 20% of the home's value upon purchase. It allows borrowers to make smaller down payments, making it possible for them to buy a home sooner since they don't have to save up as much money. Unlike MIP that is associated with an FHA loan, there is no upfront premium to pay with a conventional loan. In addition, PMI can be cancelled when the homeowner has sufficient equity in the property (usually 20-22 percent), either through appreciation or principal reduction.

Conventional 97

The Conventional 97 program requires a minimum 3 percent down payment, based on the lower of the home's appraised value or purchase price. On a $150,000 house, this translates to a down payment of $4,500 (3%), compared to $5,250 on an FHA (3.5%). In addition to the other benefits of a conventional loan mentioned above, (no upfront premium and the ability to cancel PMI with 20% equity), down payment funds can often be gifted from third parties.

If a borrower has a high enough credit score (680+), this is a far better loan than the FHA.

Fixed Rate vs. Adjustable

Fixed rate or adjustable refers to the interest rate, which can either remain the same throughout the life of the loan or change periodically. Fixed and adjustable rates are discussed below.

Fixed Rate

A fixed-rate mortgage has an interest rate that never changes. This means, unlike an adjustable-rate mortgage, borrowers are protected from higher monthly mortgage payments if interest rates suddenly rise. If mortgage rates drop, however, they do not benefit from the lower rate unless they refinance.

Even though the interest rate is fixed, the amount that a borrower will pay depends on the mortgage term. The most common terms are 30, 20, and 15 years. The 30-year mortgage is the most popular because it has the lowest monthly payment. The tradeoff is that the loan overall costs a lot more because the borrower is paying extra interest for ten or fifteen years. Additionally, the interest rate of a 30-year mortgage is typically higher than with a shorter term.

If your buyer is interested in a shorter-term loan but concerned about the higher payment, they can go with the 30-year mortgage and make additional principal payments to reduce the life of the loan. Making one extra payment per year will reduce the life of a 30-year mortgage by 8 years!

Adjustable-Rate Mortgages

ARMs are attractive to some because the initial rate is low, which allows the borrower to qualify for a larger loan. They are risky because the mortgage interest rate (and therefore the mortgage payment) changes frequently over the life of the loan. Some are structured so that interest rates can more than double in just a few years. If your buyer doesn't plan to live in a property long enough for the rates to rise, than an ARM might be a good choice. Otherwise, especially given today's low interest rates, they should stick with a fixed-rate mortgage.

USDA/Rural Housing Loans

USDA loans are insured by the Department of Agriculture. The most notable feature is their option for "no money down" or "100% financing." The purpose of the loan is to spur development of rural areas, and both the property and the buyer must quality for USDA financing. Beyond that, they are very similar to other types of loans.

With the exception of VA financing, USDA loans are really the only source of no money down financing these days. Why? Because when a homeowner doesn't have any skin in the game (home equity), there is a much higher chance that they will walk away from their mortgage and go into foreclosure. Most lenders are no longer comfortable with that level of risk. In addition, no money down means the buyer is rolling their closing costs into the loan and it will take them years to build up any equity. If they can no longer afford their payments, and they don't have enough equity in the property to cover their selling expenses, they are stuck. They have no choice but to walk away from their mortgage.

Buying a home in a USDA neighborhood is a risk, even if your buyer doesn't obtain a USDA loan. A large number of foreclosures brings down the value of the entire neighborhood. The neighborhood might be beautiful when the buyer move in, but as time goes on and their neighbors begin to neglect and ultimately lose their homes, it will change. The charming neighborhood and the value of their home will be diminished when 50% of their neighbors abandon their homes.

There is a reason that buyers must be enticed (or bribed) to move out to rural areas. These neighborhoods are far from everything, which means resale can be difficult. The pool of potential buyers in a rural area is much smaller than in neighborhoods that are closer to modern conveniences. Proceed with caution if your buyer plans to buy a home this way.

Your Buyer's Loan Step-by-Step

The following is a description of what happens, step-by-step, after your buyer chooses a lender and completes their loan application:

1. **Documentation is Ordered** - Within twenty-four hours of application, their lender will order a credit report, appraisal, verifications of employment and funds to close, and any other supporting documentation that is necessary.

2. **Wait for Documentation** - After your buyer submits their supporting documentation, the loan officer checks for any potential problems and requests additional items as needed. It can take two or three weeks for all the items to be received.

3. **Loan Submission** - Once all the necessary documentation is in, the loan officer reviews the current programs to ensure your buyer gets the best rate and terms possible. The loan processor then puts the loan package together and submits it to the underwriter for approval.

4. **Loan Approval** - Loan approval generally takes anywhere from 24 to 72 hours. All parties are notified of the approval and any loan conditions that must be received before the loan can close. The loan approval is the beginning of the closing process.

5. **Documents are Created** - Within one to three days after the loan approval, the loan documents (including the note and deed of trust) are completed and sent to the title company. The escrow officer calls the borrowers to come in when the papers are ready for final signature. At this time, the borrowers are told how much money they will need to bring in to close the loan.

6. **Funding** - Once all parties have signed the loan documents, they are returned to the lender, who reviews the package. If all the forms have been properly executed, the check is issued to fund the loan.

7. **Recording** - When the title company receives the funding check from the lender, they make the lender's security for the loan a matter of public record. They do this by recording the note and deed of trust at the county recorder's office. Escrow is now officially closed and the house belongs to your buyers!